GUY R...
WITH MONICA HOOVER

STACKING
the DECK

What Happens When We Believe
God Wants It More Than We Do

I've always been a fan of listening for God's direction before engaging energy and resources to accomplish what I believe to be His purposes. In *Stacking the Deck*, Pfanz and Hoover demonstrate the pitfalls of following human reasoning and the dramatic potential available to the church when God plans our steps. Drawing from experience in the local church and from biblical examples, the authors show the practical implications of human vs. divine strategy.

Pastors, pastoral staffs, and congregations will benefit from *Stacking the Deck*. Readers will find simple truths communicated in a profound way to challenge and edify their walk with Jesus. This is a must read for anyone seeking to avoid the perils of human reasoning as a substitute for God's direction.

—Gary Benedict, President of the Christian & Missionary Alliance Denomination

Influential platforms and super star up-front performers aren't necessary to create an atmosphere where everyone in the church feels valued for *more* than their attendance and financial support. The story of MAC is a story of a community that continues to wrestle with the challenge to value every person's personal worth and call to ministry. *Stacking the Deck* is a story worth reading, there is much to be learned here.

—Frank Tillapaugh, author of *Unleashing the Church*

GUY PFANZ
WITH MONICA HOOVER

STACKING
the DECK

What Happens When We Believe
God Wants It More Than We Do

SMALL VOICE
PUBLISHING

Muncie, Indiana

All Scripture quotations, unless otherwise indicated, are taken from the NEW AMERICAN STANDARD BIBLE®, Copyright © 1960, 1962, 1963, 1968, 1971, 1972, 1973, 1975, 1977, 1995 by The Lockman Foundation. Used by permission.

Verses marked NIV are taken from the HOLY BIBLE, NEW INTERNATIONAL VERSION®. Copyright © 1973, 1978, 1984 International Bible Society. Used by permission of Zondervan. All rights reserved.

The Message. Copyright 1993, 1994, 1995, 1996, 2000, 2001, 2002. Used by permission of NavPress Publishing Group.

Printed in the United States of America
15 14 13 12 11 10   7 6 5 4 3 2 1

Stacking the Deck
ISBN-13: 978-0-578-05114-7
ISBN-10: 0-578-05114-7

Cover and Interior Design: Mary Jaracz

DEDICATION

For Judy, who has been there through the
success and failure of many dreams. —GP

For Shawn, who always believes. —MH

CONTENTS

FOREWORD

Reluctantly, I became a children's pastor at the age of 22. I thought that by taking the position, I was fulfilling God's call on my life. It didn't pan out. The church eventually fired me because I didn't fit the corporate mold they envisioned for my position. Four months later, I was angry and disillusioned with the church and not sure what to do next, I felt God urging me to start a small group. A few of us began to meet at Beatnik's Café—a coffee bar by day, and your regular bar by night. People kept showing up. They were hungry for the word of God and responded by getting involved. As I taught the word of God, a Buddhist owner worked the bar, hippie paraphernalia hung on the walls, and beer emblems adorned the stage. It appeared unlikely, but God was up to something in this place.

One week, a group of students wandered into our meeting. They were regular attendees of Muncie Alliance Church (MAC) located forty miles away from Beatnik's Café. I didn't see it at the time, but the Spirit was at work. Their pastor Guy Pfanz called me up a few weeks later and we set up a time to meet. I arrived ten minutes early; he arrived ten minutes late. It was then that I had a hunch we would work well together. We talked for almost two hours. At the end of our meeting, Guy invited me to join the MAC internship—without reference letters or an application. I don't even think he knew my last name!

Guy's ministry philosophy freed me to serve Jesus in the unique ways God had gifted and called me. For the first time in my life, I felt encouraged to serve Jesus without fitting into a preconceived mold. The calling and moving of the Spirit in my life was more important than my job experience or what clothes I wore on Sundays. Guy sensed God's leading in my life and trained me as I served Him.

Over the past five years, Guy's stories, callings, and passions have helped lead a group of young pastors and church planters called the Movement of Alliance Communities. We have grown from one church in Muncie to multiple churches around Indiana—and even a group in Ireland. The Spirit continues to confirm Guy's role as leader, mentor, and prophet for a generation of young pastors following Jesus in a postmodern culture.

Almost every week when we gather together to study the word, discuss business, and pray for one another, Guy has a new opportunity in the works. From purchasing buildings to taking over struggling church communities from the district, there is always something being laid at Guy's feet. The difference between Guy and other spiritual leaders I've known is this: He is not afraid to leave an opportunity untouched. If he does not sense the Spirit leading us to get involved, he won't. When he senses the Spirit guiding him to take action—he will—even against our better judgment.

Stacking the Deck will challenge you to reconsider the way churches have always operated. This book will challenge you to question the molds that have stifled the body of Jesus for too long in this American church culture. It will lead you to ask God, not for His blessings on your ministry agenda, but for His purposes to be revealed to you. *Stacking the Deck* will urge you to seek the Spirit's voice in your own ministry and obediently follow. The message in the following pages has the potential to free up parts of the church so that Jesus can lead her.

I hope Guy's words challenge you in new and profound ways. After reading his story, I hope you choose to give the church back to Jesus. I hope you experience a new freedom as the Spirit leads your life and ministry in a way similar to that of the early church. I hope you will spend less time working and more time serving Jesus in the ways He has gifted you.

May you hear the Spirit's voice and obediently follow.

—Heath Pearson, lead pastor, The 509 Community

CHAPTER 1

THE SHIFT

I entered vocational ministry somewhat empty-handed. I never received an undergraduate degree and I never attended seminary. Instead, the Jesus Movement of the 1970s supplied the bulk of my education. During these transforming years I knew I was to be a pastor and I was destined to preach the word of God. So, I set out as a hippie pastor, and in place of lectures and books, I learned from experience. All along Jesus has been faithful to teach me and my wife Judy in this way. He has shaped us and how we serve Him through His word and through our trials and errors as we serve the church.

In 1975, I pastored my first church in a town of forty people. Nine adults, five of whom were retired, composed the congregation of Lilly Chapel. When I met them, they were confronted with the possibility of shutting down the church. Whether or not their dire circumstance motivated their next decision is hard to say. But as a defense against boarding up the doors, they hired me: a twenty-one-year old, single pastor without an undergradute or seminary degree. As a hippie pastor straight out of the Jesus Movement, I couldn't imagine a church service without blue jeans and rock 'n' roll. Out of desperation, they permitted my odd requests.

On my first Sunday I remember looking around at the older generation nervously adjusting their ties as the rock band tuned up. *What have I done?* I thought. As it was too late to revamp the service, I stayed the course and preached on John 14:6. "Jesus said, 'I am the way, and the truth, and the life; no one comes to the Father but through Me.'" Five teenage girls visited Lilly for the rock 'n' roll music that Sunday, and all five accepted the message of their Savior. The slumbering hearts of the people awoke and God revived the church.

It wasn't long before a girl named Judy caught my eye. The "Jesus Music" of Larry Norman, Love Song, and Barry McGuire broke through her established ideas about worship. Familiar with choirs and hymns, these new beats and melodies unlocked a dormant piece of her heart. At a Love Song concert in Chicago, the simple lyrics of "Sometimes Alleluia" rippled over the crowd and washed over her heart. For the first time, as Judy worshiped, she emotionally engaged with God. She learned a new way of conversing with the divine, and this would become her language of choice.

Upon our marriage, she became a pastor's wife at Lilly. The congregation placed no expectations upon her as she stepped into this role. They could have preyed upon her inexperience and pressured her to lead Sunday school, keep the house spotless, and involve herself in the details of every special event on the calendar. Instead, they simply loved her and graciously supported her as she learned how to employ her God-given gifts in the church. Judy eventually found her niche as a worship leader.

By the 1980s, the Church Growth Movement proved to be the dominant force within American Christianity. Church growth proponents, while extremely passionate about the Great Commission, approached building the church through calculated and statistical means. Logically, the best place to build a large church is in a place with a large population, they explained. Church growth consultants taught that in order to build a strong church most impressively and quickly, one must scope out a city, uncover needs and concerns, and then spin the values and flavor of the church to attract the most people.

Caught up in the wave of the new movement, I hosted a church growth conference at Lilly, a chapel surrounded by cornfields and forests. During one of the sessions, the consultant—whose face had been a recent fixture on the covers of all the evangelical magazines—told us,

"Jesus didn't die for clean air and corn." I felt as though he was speaking to me and his comment tempted a piece of my restless heart. I had paid my dues in this laid-back farming community. For twelve years I had pastored a growing flock. I deserved something bigger and better. He offered me the seed of ambition. I swallowed it.

With a strong desire for advancement, I planned to move away from rural, blue-collar America to launch a church in the urban sprawl of Bloomington-Normal, Illinois. In my haste to trade in the country air for young urban professionals and a low unemployment rate, I strained relationships. I enlisted the so-called top-notch believers to join me in the plant. I left the rest of Lilly in the lurch by resigning my senior pastor position without finding a replacement. In the end, I think some were glad to see me leave.

Full of focus and energy, I expected the church plant to be a slam dunk. Instead, key plans unraveled and we lost momentum. In the place of glorious success, Judy and I were left with a crumbling marriage, a forced break from vocational ministry, and strained friendships. For five years after the church plant failed, my family and I wandered in and out of towns in search of jobs. I tried selling used cars, unsuccesfully, and was eventually fired. I took a job as a lab courier. For two years I filled in as an interim pastor at a United Methodist church. We learned tough lessons in the wreckage, but one belief I had acquired from the church growth movement clung to my heart: It was my responsibility, as a pastor, to build the church.

God was about to shift my perspective. Building upon my past—both the uplifting and the thorny parts—He prepared Judy and me for a better future.

In 1992, our opportunity to serve at Muncie Alliance Church (MAC) presented itself and we entered the interview process. For the sake of honesty, I initiated an after-church lunch meeting to clearly communicate our values pertaining to church ministry—values stemming from our numerous ministry experiences. While serving at Lilly,

Judy and I learned how God had shaped us to serve the church and this affected how we ministered to the body. Some of the values we communicated at the lunch fell in line with this divine shaping. Other values, however, were a result of my lingering ambition and perceived responsibility to lead and guide the church as I saw fit.

Our ministry values, I explained after lunch, would determine the actions and appearance of the church if they asked us to come. "If you can't accept these same ideals," I requested, "please don't invite us to serve at MAC." I hoped to bypass a miserable situation, for them and for us. They admitted they were ready for a change.

A Cause for Concern

A few months after I accepted the senior pastor position at MAC, Judy noticed a pattern. Five minutes after the service concluded, the congregation filed out into the parking lot and returned to the responsibilities of the week. Accustomed to the word and worship flowing over into fellowship on Sunday mornings, this new rhythm puzzled us. This initial observation led us to notice an overarching problem within the congregation: MAC was missing a sense of community.

Troubleshooting the problem area of community, I began creating identity groups for each segment of the church in hopes of fostering community. I recruited an elder to begin a group for retirees. A mother was found to lead MOPS. I asked a musician to think about starting a small group. We made announcements for men's and women's Bible studies.

Slowly the church grew from forty-five people to ninety. It appeared the church was finally heading in the right direction.

We weren't.

In hopes of creating a connected church, I turned MAC into a department store with a great selection of products. Congregants walked in and shopped for their preferred size, color, and brand. MAC changed on the outside, but the old problem persisted. Judy and I began to question our leadership skills. Perhaps the spiritual growth we witnessed at

Lilly was a fluke. The state of MAC caused us to stop and rethink our actions, ourselves, and our ideas about how to build a church.

Jesus would faithfully suppy answers to our questions. Over the course of the following year, a succession of unexpected events shifted our perspectives about how a church is built and who does the building.

Stack the Deck

One day in frustration I prayed, "Are You ever going to do anything here, Lord?"

Standing in the parking lot, I beckoned God to open the heavens over us. We needed His blessings. The church limped along from Sunday to Sunday and I had run out of plans to implement.

"I'm going to stack the deck," He answered.

I paused.

"Stack the deck," I echoed. The words felt foreign in my mouth. I don't have the patience for card games and rarely play—this analogy wouldn't naturally occur to me. God had answered my question, but the meaning was lost on me. "Lord, what do You mean You are going to 'stack the deck'?"

He offered no further explanation.

I mulled this over for days, always asking about the meaning of this phrase. Finally an interpretation arrived: "I'm going to bring in the right people, at the right time, to do the right things. I will build My church."

Shepherd or Hireling?

Within a year of the stacked deck encounter, I attended a Calvary Chapel conference for pastors. In one of the sessions, Bob Coy, a church planter in the Calvary movement, shared a story I will never forget. The Holy Spirit affixed Bob's words in my heart and mind so that I could neither ignore nor forget his point. When I left the conference, I sensed something similar to Bob's experience would come to pass for Judy and me as well.

According to Bob, the first time he planted a church the congregation plateaued at forty people. Throughout the first two years, as the church failed to grow and lacked excitement, he second-guessed whether or not he was cut out for the job. Discouraged, he called up his director to say they still had only forty people and he was quitting. Bob assumed he would try to talk him out of giving up.

To his surprise his director replied, "You have forty people? Do you know how many guys we have who would love to plant a church with forty people? Pack your bags, we'll have someone there in two weeks."

He was free. Or so he thought.

Not too long after, while traveling in his car, Bob tuned in to a Christian radio station. A pastor was preaching on Acts 20 and spoke of the difference between a hireling and a shepherd in the Kingdom of God.

As a shepherd, the pastor explained, Paul faithfully testified of the Gospel of grace to the Ephesians. Day and night, he selflessly encouraged those who received Christ. Paul risked everything for the development of their faith. On his journey back to Jerusalem Paul completed his last act as a shepherd. He called for the Ephesian elders to meet him. The air carried the feeling of finality because the threat of imprisonment awaited him in Jerusalem.

Under these circumstances Paul offered the Ephesians the last words they would ever receive from him face to face. "Shepherd the church," Paul requested. "Shepherd her just as I have." He reminded the elders that the Holy Spirit chose them to oversee this flock. Furthermore, Jesus shed His own blood to purchase this community of believers. "After I leave," Paul warned, "ravenous wolves will come up from among you, sparing no one in the flock."[1]

Naturally, the preacher admitted, problems will arise in the church. Paul asked these elders to commit regardless of what the future held. Even if they risked their comfort, time, and reputations, Paul asked them to stay. The elders who staved off those with selfish interests and who worked through the conflicts would display their true commitment to the body. A shepherd remains in good times and bad.

Those who run from trouble are nothing but hirelings, the radio pastor said. A hireling only does his job to get paid for his work. When asked to complete tasks beyond his job description, he balks until he's paid extra. He worries about vacation days, benefit packages, and coffee breaks. The relationship between a hireling and employer is strictly business. There is no commitment. There is no sacrifice.

"The Holy Spirit smote my heart," Bob Coy admitted to a room full of pastors. He pulled off the road and repented of his hireling attitude toward the church. His first step as a shepherd was to stay on with the church plant.

As I sat in the auditorium, the Spirit warned me that I, too, would prove whether I was a shepherd or a hireling at MAC.

Reptile Dreams

Another message arrived one Sunday when an original church member approached me with a befuddling dream he dreamt the night before. He dreamt I appeared within a circle of men from the church while alligators, snakes, and lizards attacked me. "We just stood around," he explained, "and never came to your rescue." His obvious discomfort over the dream increased as he continued. "After minutes of fighting and not knowing what else to do, you bit an alligator. It went ballistic and tore you apart. Finally, someone called an ambulance and the EMTs drove you to the hospital."

Besides the upsetting outcome, this dream caught my attention for another reason. Years before my family and I moved to Muncie, I had dreamt a dream strikingly similar to this man's. While being assaulted by reptiles, people in the church had surrounded me. In my dream, however, when a knot of poisonous snakes attacked, I didn't attempt to fight them off because it appeared pointless to try. Everything began to go dark as I surrendered, but God miraculously saved me—even though the experience pained me. This man's dream parallelled mine except for this one final detail. I took notice. I believed God was warning me not to fight back and that I would need to trust in His future protection. Through this man's dream God allowed me to see the outcome if I didn't follow Him on this point. The question remained: *What* should I not fight?

The Secret Meeting

After two years of relative calm and friendliness at MAC, the unexpected appeared one Saturday night. While I was out of town, a few of the original families in the church called a meeting at the church. Disgruntled by the changes and threatened by the growing congregation, this core group wanted to fire me.

They didn't realize, however, that Judy and my daughter Misty had stayed behind in Muncie. Returning to the parsonage after running a few errands in town, Judy noticed cars in the parking lot and children playing in the churchyard.

"Hi Misty!" one of her friends yelled from the swingset.

"Mom, can I go play?"

Judy sent her off and walked over to the church figuring she must have forgotten about a meeting that evening. *I'll just stop in to say hello,* she thought. Opening the sanctuary doors, those sitting in a circle near the altar started and gaped.

"Hi…" she replied to the silence.

"Uh…we're in a meeting here," a strained voice answered.

Tongue-tied, Judy hesitated in the doorway. Her mind grappled for a phrase to ease the tension. Finding none, she quietly turned and closed the door behind her. Uncertain of the reason for the meeting, she sensed the covert agenda meant bad news for us.

Meanwhile, Misty became privy to some unanticipated information. "They're going to fire your dad," her friends had told her. "They don't want you here anymore."

Judy phoned me in Chicago to update me on the outlook of our ministry in Muncie. I struggled to process the information. *They met in secret? Why didn't they talk to me? How did I miss this?* I'd never heard rumblings. Shocked, I hung up the phone.

On Monday I called Gerry, the district superintendent, to fill him in on the events of the weekend.

"Do you feel called to Muncie?" he asked me.

After receiving the promise of the stacked deck, I didn't hesitate. "Yeah, I do."

"Don't worry, Guy. I won't let them fire you."

"What do you mean?"

"They've run off four of the last five pastors, and the problem isn't you. It's them." He refused to give them another pastor to beat up.

"But how can you stop them from firing me?"

"If they want to play hardball, then we'll close the church and give the property to you to start over."

• • •

Conversations by the back door and in the kitchen eventually clued me in to their objections. Some were bothered by my casual attire on Sunday mornings. One couple explained since I never wore ties, their son now had a good excuse to refuse to wear one. Others criticized the casual style of worship music.

In the midst of voiced preferences, some offered constructive criticism. Two men confronted me about my department-store strategy in the church. They disapproved of my attempts to satisfy everyone's needs through a specific group. "What are you going to do next?" one of the men challenged. "Create a group for left-handed car salesmen?" He was right. Instead of the church being linked together as one unified body, we were merely coexisting in various groups.

The comments and the secret meeting put me on the defensive. Then, as if on cue, I received the Christian and Missionary Alliance denominational newsletter. The president included a timely quote attributed to a famous pastor: "Don't defend yourself. God will defend you, if you are worth defending. And if not, don't waste your time."

My friend who dreamt the reptile dream was now among the group dissatisfied with my job performance. Connecting the dreams with this quote, I received God's perspective during this trying time of living under the microscope. Don't fight. Don't defend yourself—even if you are surrounded. If I fought for my own desires I would be hauled out of MAC beaten-up and wounded. But if I surrendered myself to God's purposes for the church, He would defend me.

God was refining me—my ambition surrounding the church began to recede. *This is His church*; the truth began to burrow into my heart. I shouldn't have to manipulate her in order to make changes. Instead, Jesus would faithfully transform His bride as we followed Him. A new attentiveness accompanied my every step. Before, I had made the changes I wanted—the changes I thought were my responsibility. Now I needed to check my actions by asking, *Is this really where Jesus is leading us?* I repeatedly reminded myself: *The church doesn't belong to them; she doesn't belong to me. The church belongs to Jesus.*

Even with this new perspective, the following months were excruciating as the congregation continued to battle for ownership.

Biblically speaking, no room is given to flag-waving in the church—whether patriotic or denominational. Nationalism from the pulpit particularly infuriates me. So early on, being careful not to associate myself with it, I removed the flags from the altar and stored them in a back room. Eventually, one Sunday while Judy and I were out of town, someone returned the flags to their flanking positions. Examining my motives first, I promptly removed them.

Relational degeneration also surfaced through praise and worship. One man decided church without a choir on Sunday morning was bad enough, but he refused to sit through an Easter morning service without one. He gathered a few other people—really not enough for a proper choir—bound and determined to have a robed ensemble front and center on this special Sunday.

"Were you there when they crucified my Lord? Were you there?" His voice boomed over the rest of the choral members and interrogated the congregation. The performance had less to do with the epic showdown of good and evil and more to do with the triumph of preserving the status quo. Flush with victory, he took his seat. In the moments before I left mine, I realized a mouthful of another sermon had already been preached that morning. The congregation and I now played for opposing teams.

A Point of View on Benton Road

Starved for genuine worship and needing to duck the tension, Judy planned to attend a worship service in Indianapolis a few weeks later. She made arrangements for a couple in the area to lead a few songs in her absence. Unfortunately, the young couple never showed up. Minutes before the start of service, with the couple unreachable by phone and Judy an hour away in Indy, I made the thirty-second walk over to church in uncomfortable silence. There was only one person was left to lead the music: me.

"We'll sing a couple of songs," I directed after I explained the circumstances. I cleared my throat and started a song a capella. The faltering effort on everyone's part never quite gained enough momentum to be termed singing. I wasn't sure, but either I started the song in the wrong key or I kept dropping a beat every few measures. *I'm not going through the motions just to say we did it*, I decided.

As the first verse trailed off, I spoke up, "Hey, this isn't going to work, is it?" Moving directly into the sermon, the service finished in record time. Within a half hour of trying to start a song, I found myself back home in the parsonage.

"I'm out of here," I muttered as I slammed the door behind me. I didn't want to live in Muncie or be the pastor of MAC anymore.

Everything felt pathetic. I started toward Benton Road to walk off some frustration.

To my left, in an enclosed field, grazed a horse and donkey. In the midst of my angry thoughts I didn't notice them, but I caught their attention. They lazily rambled over for a closer look and began to walk with me. The oddness of walking down the road with a horse and donkey following me in the adjacent field was strangely comforting. My fury cracked and cooled.

I stopped to pet them. I picked grass they couldn't reach on the other side of the fence and fed them. As we continued together, I began a rhetorical conversation with God. "See, they're following me," I motioned to the animals as we played follow-the-leader. "Why won't anyone else?" I wondered aloud.

After a few minutes, we neared the edge of the field. The corral stopped them as an open road extended before me. I had the freedom to walk on.

We all have perimeters we can't cross, the Spirit spoke in my heart. As negative as this might sound, it didn't strike me so. At MAC, two different sets of values and experiences with God presented themselves; neither were wrong or sinful, but each had different perimeters. *They've walked with you as far as they can go. They can't go any further. It's okay.*

Later that same week we received a call from Pat, a friend from Lilly Chapel. She explained she saw a vision of me leaving the house, slamming the door behind me, and saying "I'm out of here." Fearing I had left Judy, she called to check up on us. I assured her our marriage was fine but the church was not. The phone call convinced Judy and me the happenings at MAC had not escaped God's attention. Sobered to know He was moving others to pray for us, we realized He was orchestrating events behind the scenes. Hope sprung up in our hearts. Order could grow from the problems and inconveniences we viewed as chaos. Instead of a grocery list of reasons to leave MAC, we now had one big reason to stay.

Audience of One

In choosing to stay, we wanted to try to ease the uncomfortable state of affairs. We decided to meet with those in the group of dissatisfied members in hopes of reaching some compromises. We brought our paper, we listened, we made lists. After meeting with two families, finding incompatible ideas and requests I personally could not fulfill, I knew it would be impossible to find common ground.

Sitting in the living room, reviewing the list of responses from the meetings, Judy felt cornered. She understood what everyone wanted and she was willing to take everyone's opinion into account. She viewed them as people, not as obstacles. But no one had the same idea of what it would take to have a satisfying church experience. Leaning back on the couch, she thought to herself, *We feel called to MAC and they feel called to MAC. But we are never going to mesh.*

At that moment, the Lord cut through her hopelessness and responded. *Live for an audience of one. I'm calling you to lay down the list and to live to please Me.*

Cognitively, she knew the pleasure of the Lord trumped the pleasure of people. For the first time, however, this truth penetrated her heart. She found the strength to lay down the list despite the unhappiness it would cause others.

The Spider Web

Just as God had tailored a reassurance for Judy, He planned one for me as well. I woke up to fog one Sunday, my mind turning over the future of the church. I remember thinking how the congregation wasn't solely responsible for the uproar. For one, I had been ambitious. Had it seeped into other areas unawares? I had also been wrong to treat the church like a department store, as a few had pointed out to me. Possibly the rest of what they were saying had merit as well. God had told me not to fight. Maybe I was to yield to their desires.

Walking over to the bay window in the parsonage, I looked out. The thick air played tricks on my eyes, concealing the tree, the yard, and the road so I could neither focus nor perceive depth. "God," I mused, "maybe I'm too busy trying to be cool to be what You want me to be. Maybe I ought to just put on a tie, fire up the organ, and bring on the choirs. We'll do things their way—at least then I'll still be able to preach Your word."

A movement caught my attention in the foreground. Against a backdrop of white, a black spider appeared. The welcomed focal point dropped down from the overhang outside the bay window. Suspended in front of my nose, I watched him.

"God, what should I do to follow You?"

The spider moved up and down the silken thread distracting me from prayer. Without pause, he connected each strand efficiently.

My mind ran over more questions. "Have You called me specifically to MAC or have You called me to the city of Muncie?"

If He would just answer this question, I thought, I would know how to order my steps. If He called me to this church, then I'd put on a tie and play it their way. If He called me to this community, then I'd study the demographics of Muncie and modify the church in a relevant way.

He didn't answer me this time.

While I stood there, a delicate network began to emerge before me. Once arbitrary, the mess became orderly. Impressively, this spider had known what he was doing from the start. I gave in to the diversion. "God, how does this spider know how to create a precise web?"

"This spider is doing what I put within him to do. He doesn't think about it," He replied.

"Huh," I concluded, thinking that was nice.

Missing the application of the analogy unfolding before me, I repeated myself, "God, what have You called me to do?"

He responded, "Guy, I shaped you and formed you in the '70s and I made you who you are today. I put within you the ability to do what

I want done here at MAC. You're about to give up and throw away all that I have arranged."

Soon after, I walked to the church from the parsonage as the sun burnt off the fog. Up in a tree I noticed another spider web. The sun had transformed the dewy concentric circles into strands of diamonds and the brilliance caught my eye. In my heart the Lord asked, "What do you think of this one?"

"It's beautiful, Lord."

"I put it there for you to see today..."

Thirty seconds later, with the key in my hand to unlock the church, God continued, "...and I'm going to put a church here for the world to see."

Suddenly, it hit me: *I'm a spectator.* Ever since the secret meeting, I thought MAC had been suspended in gridlock. I had incorrectly viewed the congregation and myself like two teams, battling it out on a playing field. In my mind, no team had advanced toward victory because we were both applying equal pressure. For instance, I busied myself with duties such as creating a connected community and promoting casual dress and music. I thought the reason my actions had failed to affect the church was because of the congregation's defensive tactic to maintain the status quo.

When God said He would build the church, I finally realized the congregation and I were spectators, not opposing teams. I had left out Jesus. He was fighting for His church. Accepting my seat in the stands, so to speak, I reflected upon the last two years at MAC. Slowly, the ways in which God had been affecting change upon His church began to emerge. All along He had been building His church—I just couldn't see it on the surface. He had carefully arranged messages about stacked decks and shepherds and hirelings to bring new foundational perspectives about His church. He set up circumstances years in advance—such as my friendship with Pat, my reptile dream, and a district superintendent who would keep our place at MAC secure—to prepare Judy and me to see His point in Muncie.

What was His point? The congregation and the pastor aren't responsible to build the church. Christ will build His church.

Eventually the congregation found out the district stood behind Judy and me and the malcontents left and scattered within a few short weeks. Shocked their power had been diffused, one man flashed the remaining weapon in his arsenal. "See if you can make it without our money!" he sputtered in a final phone conversation.

Interestingly enough, those who left attended separate churches. Only unified against the changes Judy and I brought with us, their commonality quickly dissolved outside of MAC. Thinking back on my walk down Benton Road, I knew God still cared for these people. They had purposes elsewhere. Attending churches as newcomers, perhaps they would experience freedom as they released their sense of guardianship over the church.

Nearly sixty percent of the church left as my third year of pastoring MAC began. Our finances took a hit after the major exodus. In an effort to stay afloat financially, we sold the grand piano and the trailer that served as extra Sunday school rooms. The district paid off the debt owed on the building and suspended our payments, without interest, until we could afford them again.

After all those measures, we still ran out of money. During a congregational meeting called to discuss additional budget cuts, Judy and I reduced our annual salary to ease the financial stress upon the church.

"I suppose this means you'll be leaving us to find a church who can support you and your family," a worried woman commented after the meeting.

"No," I replied. "We're staying." God had called us to MAC.

• • •

Months later, in a conversation with my Father, I brought up my last unanswered question. "God you were so gracious to me with the spider web analogy—permitting me to do what you had put within me to do—why didn't you speak to my question about being called to the church or the community?"

God finally answered the dangling question. *I didn't call you to this church or to this community. I called you to follow Me.*

Judy and I had learned "Christ is the head of the body" by rote. To us, this foundational truth was just a filler in our Christian jargon, a pat response we repeated instead of a fact that ordered our steps. We needed new words.

To bring us to this point, God cleared away our notions of pastoral and congregational responsibility to build the church by jarring our routine with struggle. Confusion followed, melting away our elementary ideas about the church. The bare space provided room for a revelation. When we saw His power and desire to build the church, our perspective underwent a shift. Moses experienced a shift at the burning bush. Isaiah experienced the same standing in the temple in the sixth chapter of his book. We too were on the brink of receiving a revelation. Our revelation would change our perspectives about the bride. We learned He is able and desires to build His church. He wants it more than we do. And because of this, we are free from driving the church to success on our own. In the place of "Christ is the head of the body," He gave us new words:

I'm going to stack the deck.
The church belongs to Jesus.
I called you to follow Me.

Christ will build His church.

Questions for Reflection

1. What does the phrase *Christ is the head of the church* mean to you?

2. How has your ambition ever caused you to run ahead of God?

3. Do you feel a sense of guardianship over the church?

4. What expectations have you placed on your pastor? Do these expectations push him into the role of a shepherd or hireling?

CHAPTER 2

TWO CITIES

Christ will build His church. I finally believed it after the events of my transforming year. Even better, God had graciously given me promises to hold on to. Now what? I was ready to move forward in faith. But to where?

Doesn't this sound like Abraham? Indulge me as we take a closer look at his life. Put yourself in his sandals because when you believe God will build His church, you will identify with the life of Abraham more deeply than ever before.

Let's begin by flipping back one chapter in Genesis in order to understand the context of Abraham's story. Abraham's life offers a powerful alternative to one that came before him: Nimrod.

Nimrod's Babylon

Nimrod said, "Come, let us build for ourselves a city…and make for ourselves a name."[2] A group numbering in the thousands settled on the plains of Shinar and staked its territory with an imposing ziggurat, or temple tower, visible from afar. Nimrod's strategy for greatness guided the people and together they built the city of Babylon.

The impressive city caught the eye of God, and brought Him down from heaven to take a closer look. "Now nothing which they purpose to do will be impossible for them," He remarked.[3] The city of Babylon proved humankind's nearly endless potential. With Nimrod's vision and leadership, the Babylonians displayed self-sufficiency and power, and garnered the attention of others. Whatever the citizens of Babel needed, they could collectively figure out and do themselves. Whatever they desired, they could make it happen. Who needed to trust in a distant God?

The Second City

Directly after showcasing Nimrod's Babylon, in Genesis 12 the writer highlights a second city. In contrast to the city made by man, this second city begins by a revelation from God.

Abraham grew up in the city of Ur located in the region of Babylonia. The culture of Babylon, evidenced by the ziggurats dotting the landscape, would have affected his hometown.[4] But God wanted to build a city contrary to the misguided strivings of Babylon. He reveals His overarching plan to Abraham with this famous promise:

> Go forth from your country,
> And from your relatives
> And from your father's house,
> To the land which I will show you;
> And I will make you a great nation,
> And I will bless you,
> And make your name great;
> And so you shall be a blessing;
> And I will bless those who bless you,
> And the one who curses you I will curse.
> And all the families of the earth will be blessed.
> (Genesis 12:1-3)

Unlike Nimrod's clear-cut plan, Abraham's divine revelation would cause him to live in ambiguity. He became a strange person leaving for a strange land that he would see at an unknown time. On this journey, even his daily routines would break down until they became useless and forgotten. To follow this revelation, Abraham abandoned the ease of the known—the comfort of living in the midst of the familiar—as he journeyed into this nameless place. Not quite a drifter, he was not quite settled either.

But God promised, "I will make your name great." God used an arrangement of words catching Abraham's attention and reminding him of an old story—the story of Nimrod. A handful of Abraham's forefathers who witnessed the rise and fall of Babylon lived into the span of his life. They must have recounted to him the tale of Nimrod—his failed quest to build a city and a name for himself. God's promise, however, altered Nimrod's words in a holy way. Rearranged, these ancient words now laid the responsibility of greatness upon an almighty diety. *God* would create a new city, and a great one it would be.

In faith, Abraham set out and looked for a city whose architect and builder was God.

Chazon vision

Abraham, the father of our faith, had no idea where he was going. But this is often viewed as unacceptable in our contemporary churches. If a pastoral search committee asked a candidate, "What is your vision for this church?" do you think he would be hired if he answered, "I don't know?" We've come to expect a plan of action and Proverbs 29:18 is our favorite verse to quote in defense of vision statements: "Where there is no vision, the people perish."

Unfortunately, in defense of our plans we've inserted an incorrect definition of vision into this verse. Proverbs 29:18 has nothing to do with man's vision and everything to do with God's revelation to man. We've traded the vision displayed by Abraham's life, a revelation from God, for the vision displayed by Nimrod: excellent foresight in an earthly world.

King Solomon wrote Proverbs 29 and chose the Hebrew word *chazon* for verse 18. Translated into English, *chazon* simply means "vision" or "revelation." But to better understand the meaning of this word, let's look to the place where *chazon* first appears, 1 Samuel 3:1. "Now the boy Samuel was ministering to the Lord before Eli. And word from the Lord was rare in those days; visions were infrequent." In this verse, the infrequency of visions (*chazon*) parallels the rare appearance of a "word from the Lord." Based on simple grammar, *chazon* points to revelations from the Lord, not real-world acumen. *Chazon* is about divine communication, divine guidance, and divine circumstances that bring about divine plans.

Chazon also appears in 1 Chronicles 17. King David longs for the Ark of the Covenant to rest in a majestic dwelling; it seemed audacious to live in his house of cedar while the Lord dwelled in a tent. His desire to build a house for the Lord sprung from the best intentions. Nathan urged King David to go along with the plan. God, however, had something different in mind. That night a word from God visited Nathan and explained that God chose David's son Solomon, not David, to construct a house for the Lord. Nathan relayed the *chazon*-vision to David the next morning and David followed God's lead. Interestingly enough, this passage illustrates an example of God's vision directly conflicting with the earnest plan of a godly man—a plan that even received the initial blessing of a prophet.

The second half of Proverbs 29:18 counsels that where there is no *chazon*, "the people perish." Some versions use the phrase "are unrestrained." Looking once more to the Hebrew language, the English word "unrestrained" comes from the Hebrew word *para*, meaning: to let go, let loose, ignore, let alone. The first mention of *para* appears twice in Exodus 32:25: "Moses saw that the people where *running wild* and that Aaron had let them *get out of control* and so become a laughingstock to their enemies."[5] The Israelites lost patience when Moses tarried on the mountaintop. Misinterpreting God's silence for His absence, the restless Israelites left God by the wayside. Instead of bending the knee, they decided to lead themselves. The results were disastrous—remember the golden calf?

Ironically enough, by employing Proverbs 29:18, "Where there is no vision, the people perish" to defend our vision statements, the church lives out the truth of this verse, but not in the positive way she expects. When we act as though our plans are necessary to keep us from shipwrecking our churches, we crowd out God. Just like the Israelites at the foot of Mount Sinai, we let go of God, we release the divine, and we ignore Him. Left without a *chazon*-vision, we become spiritually weak. If this weren't bad enough, just like the Israelites, instead of witnessing the true and living God, we become a laughingstock to those who rise up against us. Eugene Peterson's word choice in *The Message* helps us understand the correct meaning of this verse: "If people can't see what God is doing, they stumble all over themselves; but when they attend to what he reveals, they are most blessed." [6]

Instead of asking ourselves what is our vision for our churches and ministries, we should be asking: How are we attending to His revelation?

Attending to His Revelation

When God reveals Himself to people, they change their perspectives. A person's brush with the divine—whether it's through words, an image, or his present circumstances—corrects the ideas he has about himself and the ideas he has about God. When God reveals Himself, the initial response is humility and the sense of having nothing worthwhile to offer. What follows is the assurance of God's plan and His power to bring about this plan through the lives of people and divine circumstances. The holy encounter repositions this person and becomes a launching pad for a reordered life—a life attending to what He reveals. Abraham wasn't the only one to experience this progression. Here are a few others who followed *chazon*:

While shepherding his father-in-law's flock of sheep, Moses noticed a burning bush. Wondering why the shrub didn't collapse into an ash heap, he walked over to take a closer look. Little did he know he was about to meet God. Calling out from the midst of the fire God unveiled his destiny, but Moses quickly protested: "Who am I, that I should go to Pharaoh, and that I should bring the sons of Israel out of Egypt?"[7] A valid question. Moses possessed no power or credentials to sway this powerful man, and public speaking wasn't his forte. In a lengthy conversation, God spoke to all of Moses's fears and questions. One day Moses went for a walk, encountered the great I AM, and then left Midian to free his brothers in Egypt.

Isaiah saw the Lord sitting on a throne, lofty and exalted, where Seraphim flitting above were compelled to repeat, "Holy, holy, holy, is the Lord of hosts. The whole earth is full of His glory."[8] When the voice from the temple spoke, the earth quaked and the temple filled with smoke. Isaiah's response: "I am ruined because I am a man of unclean lips!"[9] He encountered God. The discrepancy between the holy and his sinful self shook him physically in grief and despair. A fiery coal was brought from the brazen alter. As it touched his lips, the Lord cleansed him from his sins. Then God asked for an ambassador for the Father, Son, and Holy Spirit. Isaiah was ready and willing to fulfill the role. Upon experiencing the supernatural, Isaiah's response moved from "Woe is me" to "I will go!"

Saul met God on the road to Damascus and became the Apostle Paul—a pompous Christian-killer turned humble servant of the Gospel. Not only did Paul bring to the Jews the very message of Christ he attempted to stomp out but he also unveiled God's mysterious plan of salvation to the Gentiles—a people group he abhorred in his former life as a Pharisee.

Attending to what God reveals results in life and the construction of something lasting. We see this as we observe the lives of Moses, Isaiah, Paul, and in Abraham as he looks for a city whose architect is God.

The Results of the Two Visions

Revisiting the narratives of Nimrod and Abraham, the opposing visions of these men carried them to two very different destinations.

Nimrod dismissed God as a delusion not to be trusted and instead depended upon his own foresight and plans. In the end, his proactive measures to build a city to keep from being scattered failed miserably. The people never completed the city of Babylon because God scattered them about the face of the whole earth with new languages, hindering any efforts to regroup.

At first glance, it appears foolish to say Abraham's city fares better than Nimrod's. Abraham's life ends after fourteen chapters without the expected crescendo. He died in faith without ever receiving the promise. After living uncomfortably, exposed to the elements and danger, he passed away before seeing his descendants become as innumerable as the stars, without seeing his fourth generation inhabit the Promised Land, without seeing how God blessed the families of the earth because of him.[10] Reading his rap sheet and looking at the bottom line, it appears God tricked Abraham.

Under the surface, however, beyond the recorded doings of his life, something else was happening. Those near Abraham knew he did not leave this world empty-handed as he attended to God's revelation. Perhaps Isaac and Jacob noticed these deeper happenings while their father was alive. There was peace in his movements, even as a sojourner. They clearly saw the consciousness of God's provision in Abraham's eyes. He possessed a humble confidence as an old man that made others feel as though he knew something, some secret that allowed him to live beyond the present. Those near him in the end knew this secret: he was on familiar terms with God. He recognized God's voice. He experienced the intimacy of covenant with Him. In life he developed a friendship with the great I AM who was a shield to him; his very great reward.[11] All these characteristics of Abraham are the results of following the Lord's *chazon*.

In the end, God didn't forget His promises to Abraham and his descendants. Time proved God's words. The Israelites became a mighty nation in Egypt. Later, they moved into the Promised Land. Later still, of Abraham's lineage the Christ was born blessing all in the earth who call upon His name. And the city, the heavenly city that God is preparing for him and his descendants is still yet to come—and Abraham will view it with his own eyes.[12]

The Workmanship of God

In contrast to Abraham's godly characteristics, we have the profanity of the Laodiceans of Revelations 3, the ultimate result of a church who ascribes to Nimrod's vision: "I am rich, and have become wealthy, and have need of nothing."[13] Despite the Laodiceans' claims, one flaw greatly compromises their boasting. They are blind. Instead of being the happy, healthy, growing, rich, poster-child church they profess to be, Jesus calls them wretched, miserable, poor, blind, and naked. All their wealth, all their self-sufficiency, and all their capabilities push Jesus right out the front door of His church. Outside He stands, knocking and calling out so someone will hear Him and invite Him back in.

If only the Laodiceans would open the door and allow Christ to come in and lead, they would witness Him building a church that far surpasses their best efforts. However, the best efforts of man—riches, precedent, strategies, and the like—often win out because they are easy to observe and to follow. The trouble with opening the door to Christ (and keeping Him inside His church) is that His workmanship is oftentimes difficult to see. Like in the case of Abraham, sometimes when we let Him lead, it appears nothing is happening.

But wait anyway. Take a cue from Abraham.

Abraham wanted to live in a city built and designed by God. He rejected the alternative of Nimrod's Babylon and waited. He waited even when it was uncomfortable. Abraham placed his faith in God instead of the final destination; he embraced the promise and moved forward. In faith, he tore down and reconstructed the family tents again and again, believing one day it would be for the last time. In faith, he exchanged the comfort of permanence for life on the road. To the end, Abraham never returned to Ur, confirming he did not seek a country of his own.[14] Finally, at the dawn of eternity the New Jerusalem appears, the city God created. Abraham's momentary light affliction of walking through life by faith in response to God's revelation produced an observable, eternal weight of glory beyond all comparison.[15]

• • •

We in the church can choose to attend to what God reveals. We can join the ranks of Moses, Paul, and Abraham and invite Christ to come in and lead our churches. If we do, we will end up with His workmanship, something to which the works of man can never aspire. Yet so often we settle for the works of man.

Questions for Reflection

1. How have you defined *vision* in Proverbs 29:18?

2. How are you attending to His revelation?

CHAPTER 3

WHOSE CHURCH IS IT ANYWAY?

In order for us to truly embrace the idea that God wants to build the church more than we do, we must scrutinize the way we handle ministry in our churches. The ministry philosophies in the following pages are grouped into three stereotypical churches: the traditional church, the professional church, and the consumer-driven church. Each crowds Christ out of His church in some way, just like the Laodicean church. This chapter might be uncomfortable to read, but if we truly want to follow the Holy Spirit in our churches, then the practices on the following pages must die.

The Traditional Church

The traditional church borrows from the democratic model and exists *by the people for the people*. I grew up in a traditional church and my first pastorate in the early '70s was a traditional church. The church attendance roster hovered in the teens, so pulling together during uncertain times forged deep, strong ties between us all. Even slightly embarrassing anecdotes are sentimental to me when I think back on that church. Located in a extremely rural and extremely poor part of the Midwest during the 1970s, our church bathroom was actually an outhouse. During my stint there, we built a bathroom addition onto the church. Three of us hand-dug a fourteen-by-eight-foot well, hauling the dirt up with buckets and ropes, until we hit water suitable enough for indoor plumbing.

I also remember leading one of my first congregational meetings in this traditional church. Nearly fifty people were in attendance and toilet paper had made the agenda. Around and around the circle we went, listing our options. Should we purchase it in four-packs or by the case? How could we best steward the money God gave us? It seemed purchasing it by the case would be more cost-effective. Yet, where would we store the paper once we had ordered so much of it? Once we closed that order of business, we moved on to the next: our mice problem. This meeting became emotional as we discussed poison or traps. How would the mice suffer less?

Generally speaking, traditional churches discuss everything, weighing the merits of every option in every situation, at times even in the face of a life-threatening situation. During a Sunday night Bible study, members of a traditional church just south of Muncie received a call from a man claiming a bomb would detonate in five minutes. Instead of leaving the church immediately, the Bible study members deliberated for *forty minutes*—Was the call a prank? Should we treat this seriously?—before they finally decided to call the police. The church could have exploded as they weighed their options. (Ultimately, no one was injured.)

The Trappings of Democracy

On decisions regarding toilet paper and mice, I rarely cared which way the verdict went. Twenty years later and in a different traditional church as an interim pastor, I did care about an outcome. A ministry idea of mine went to vote, and I lost. At the time, our church hosted twelve-step programs, yet the faces I saw on Tuesday nights rarely showed up on Sunday mornings. God was doing some amazing work in the basement and I wanted those in recovery to rub shoulders with the group up in the sanctuary on Sunday mornings (mostly to the benefit of those on the first floor). The idea was to have the congregation host a dinner in honor of those in the recovery groups, to serve them, to encourage them, and to show them our respect for their perserverance through a tough time in life. The board voted against it. No reasons were given when the idea was shot down, although I had my speculations. It was infuriating to be told no by those who did not carry my burden.

This "defeat" caused me to wonder. This sort of thing happened all the time. Other pastors I knew talked about being stopped from carrying out a call because of the decision of a majority. I often heard congregant complaints of the same variety. When I thought about the logic and the preference of the majority determining the course of the church—instead of the prompting of the Holy Spirit for instance—I became increasingly uncomfortable. As a church, we had been shaped by that vote against the banquet. We became a more safe and preservative church that carried the fingerprints of the dissenting voters. Should a church's destiny depend upon membership agreement? How often does the Holy Spirit lead where the faithful do not want to go—to where we are not comfortable?

What would have happened if Abraham had turned to Sarah,[16] Lot, and their servants after God had spoken the promises to him in the land of Haran and asked, "So what do you think? Shall we move out from our country, leave our family, and travel to a land that I've only been promised about?" I imagine Sarah was full of questions: *Where are we going? Have you seen this place before? How long will we be gone?* I'm sure Lot was doubtful. Traveling into the territory of the Hittites, Canaanites, and Amorites would be asking for a fight.

Certainly the majority, out of common sense and the noble pursuit of protecting a family, would have voted to sit still exactly where they were.

When a church is run by the people for the people, we often opt for the less risky course of action. But without risk, there is no need for faith.

The Primary Group

Once at a local pastors' meeting, I asked a Baptist pastor how the work was going.

"Well, brother," he replied, "we are only two funerals away from revival." He pronounced it "re-VAL-val." In other words, two more funerals would break up the power source within his church and God would finally have the space to do what He wanted; He could bring re-VAL-val.

In traditional churches, there is always a group that "runs" the church. Their authority stems from past good works, money, seniority, or family name. In my experience, as the core group continues to wield their power and grow accustomed to power's effects, they start taking ownership of the church in subtle ways, heightening their sense of obligation and responsibility until it becomes blatantly obvious to others who is in charge. The church becomes their possession to protect. This is a problem. Past actions, even if they were selfless, sacrificial, and pleasing to the Lord, should never translate into the unquestioned right to shape the future of the church. This job belongs to the Holy Spirit.

This idea of a church by the people for the people also deeply affects the role of a pastor. He finds himself in a weakened position; his hands are tied when the congregation or a few power brokers hold most of the control within the church. Continually responding to the peoples' will reduces his role of shepherd into that of a chaplain—or in the worst of cases—a hireling. Those in the congregation view him as a means to serve the current system. They pay him to preach, teach, visit, counsel, marry, and bury.

A Red Tape Strangling

When the pastor is a hireling and the congregation, elder board, or primary group runs the show, Christ's body becomes a slow-moving, behemoth of a bureaucracy. Much like the toilet paper and mice issues at Lilly Chapel, endless discussion or endless rounds of committee approval keep a church moving at a snail's pace. What a waste of time! As a bi-vocational pastor, I install coffee bars, and some of my jobs happen to be in these churches. From a sales point of view, it is much easier to close a deal with certain denominations. Recently while speaking to a Presbyterian client, I commented how grateful I was that she wasn't a United Methodist, given their notoriety for making every initiative pass through multiple committees. She chuckled, and replied, that at her church the coffee bar needed to gain approval by "only two" committees.

Even a church insider is required to jump through these same hoops. If someone senses a call to begin a new ministry, she must first become skilled at landing space on a committee agenda. Most likely, these committees meet once a month. As she talks with the committee chair, she finds out she just missed getting on the agenda for the meeting scheduled for July. "Oh, and in August," he replies, "we won't be meeting because the Millers will be out of town. So, in September why don't you stop in and tell us what's on your heart?"

When the Holy Spirit moves one of His children to fulfill her unique part in the body of Christ, it is a shame that we would waste any time in testing that leading (outside of a committee), and if the idea is found worthy, enabling and helping her along as she walks in obedience to God. Instead of expecting God to move and feeling excitement as we watch God's plans unfold, those ready to follow God are discouraged and asked to stand in line. A church laden with red tape is equally burdened with the frustrated who give up, leave, or at the very worst, die spiritually while sitting in the pew. A bureaucracy stunts growth and pushes Jesus outside His church.

In a traditional church, the Holy Spirit's wind still moves His children to act. They're just strangled by red tape.

• • •

These flawed profiles of traditional churches are found across the country. Pastors and worshipers alike wonder, *Is this what it's supposed to look like?* Some doubt it and leave to build or join something new. A church where a pastor can lead unshackled by the congregation becomes the dream of a beaten-up traditional pastor. His frustration catapults him into an unhealthy balance of wanting to call the shots himself. When a congregation hands ownership of the church over to the pastor, the result is the professional church.

The Professional Church

The professional church borrows from the American corporate culture. Believers in this type of church choose to rely on human ability and mental prowess instead of harnessing the power of the Holy Spirit. This church interprets the word "vision" found in Proverbs 29:18 as the plans and dreams of a man. She embraces corporate vision instead of *chazon*-vision. By doing so, believers have stepped out from under Christ's headship and into the earthly arena of human achievement. A professional church believes they want ministry to happen more than

God and they drive it through marketing, by running demographic studies, and formulating five-year plans.

The Top-Down Approach

When I interviewed for my current senior pastor position at MAC, I wrote out my vision and five-year plan for the church and passed it out to the interviewing board. None of my plans contradicted scripture and most could fall under the commands to fulfill the Great Commission and train faithful men and women in the faith. Many other pastors claim the same thing about their vision statements and goals for the church. Yet, all this goodness distracts as a sickness slips into the church: The pastor now sits in the seat of control and the local church becomes *his* possession. He is a man with a plan and his staff and congregation view him as a sort of Chief Executive Officer of their church. He is free to lead and guide his staff and congregation based upon his human vision. The vision drives the focus and activities of the church and sifts out anything contrary to the mission statement.

A corporate definition of success invades the church as well. As all competent CEOs must prove their worth through a growing business, so does a CEO pastor with growing attendance and budgets. When I meet people or other pastors for the first time, after the general friendly exchange, a familiar question often surfaces. "So, how many people do you have in your congregation?" People look at you differently if you answer 5000 rather than 50. The higher the number, the more interested people are in "your secret." They think, *Whoa, he must be doing something right because God is really blessing him.* This definition of success begs more questions: What about those without large congregations? Are they seen as less in the Kingdom of God? Do smaller churches deserve less blessing from God?

Role of Staff

Well-educated and experienced staff are the key to a professional pastor's success. A stereotypical professional church limits who gets to do ministry because their value of excellence demands perfection. This church fears the messes made by young believers who are over-zealous and have the tendency to make mistakes. The ministries of the church are determined in the staff meetings, carefully calculated, and then garnished in prayer. Any risk must be controlled because failure is unacceptable.

The congregation loses the opportunity to creatively serve in the way God calls them. Instead, they must see where they fit in. The pastor and staff insert volunteers into the open positions provided by the five-year plan. If a creative leader approaches the pastor and staff with an idea for ministry, they may listen to his ideas and might incorporate them. Yet seldom would this idea man be hired or asked to lead his ministry. These practices in a professional church eventually lead the congregation to believe they must leave ministry to the professionals.

Imported Programs

Whether the pressure for pastors to produce results stems from their ambition, the expectations of others, or a combination thereof, they are tempted to discover what brought success to other churches and synthetically duplicate it in their own. Taking inventory of his church and homing in on the weak areas, a professional pastor shops around for a ministry program. Regardless of whether a pastor buys a program, attends a conference, or purchases a franchise, security lies in the execution of a known and tested man-made plan.

Pastors with large congregations and even larger budgets will probably be able to implement the new program with relative ease. However, for pastors lacking resources, the process of implementation becomes a little tricky. These imported programs have often failed me and my friends. Pastors who develop sucessful programs usually possess the talent to run a Fortune 500 company. Those with less ability become increasingly frustrated as they try over and over to mimic the success of others. *Failure just seems to follow me*, they believe as they wonder if they are cut out to be a pastor afterall. *Did I miss the call?*

In reality, the wrong people are asking the wrong questions. The church attempting to function as a well-oiled machine should instead answer the questions: Where's the faith? Where's the necessity of prayer? Where is the space for Christ to lead, call, or stir?

The Consumer-Driven Church

I once received the following e-mail from a man who visited our church:

> Dear Muncie Alliance,
> My family visited your church this past Sunday. We come from a C&MA background and must admit I was horribly disappointed with our visit. We have recently moved and started

looking for a new church to call home. I would like to paint you a picture of our experience, so here is how I told the story to my pastor from our previous church.

We pulled out of the driveway to start our thirty-five-minute drive to the Muncie Alliance Church. We pull into this church and it has been raining and continues to do so. The very full parking lot is a once-gravel, soupy mess. We walk into church with our shoes dirty—but that is okay because there is no one in the door to greet us or that might notice our dirty shoes. NO ONE!

So we walk on in to the coffee bar. Very nice. People are mingling and talking and seeming to have a good time. The four of us walk to the entrance of the sanctuary and wait for the first service to empty. Oh, by the way—no one has spoken to us and we have probably been there a good five minutes. Once it seems like the first service crowd empties, we go in and sit toward the rear of the large sanctuary. One man (Eric) comes over, says hello, and hopes we feel welcome. He does explain that most people there are new in the past year or so.

Before the service began, our son had to go potty. In the bathroom with my wife, he asks if this will be our new church and such (he isn't very quiet if you remember children at that age). None of the other five or six ladies make any comment to her whatsoever. Maybe they were upset because there was no toilet paper in the women's restroom—they must not have been expecting anyone on a Sunday.

So our children are pretty traumatized over this new environment and our daughter makes such a commotion after the song service (which was pretty good) that she and I have to leave. While we are out in the foyer no one speaks to us. There are a few people mingling about. She and I are at the coffee bar (alone) when my wife and son come to join us. It seems that the pastor said "crap" from the pulpit and my son said, "Mommy, he can't say that!" So we left. No one asked for any information on us so that we might be contacted, nor did it seem like we were overly welcomed there. It appeared that your target audience was college students and we didn't fit into your target. It was horribly disappointing and draining. We want to come back to our home church!

We are trying to teach our children the value of church and controlling their tongue. Maybe this is not typical of your Sunday services. But if it is, please consider a few changes. People matter.

I like to hear my Father's voice through others, and I prayerfully sought to discern what He might be saying to me, or to the church that He has entrusted into my stewardship, through this e-mail.

The oversight in the women's restroom greatly embarrassed me and I was disappointed that other people besides Eric did not speak to this family. We have designated greeters stationed outside the auditorium to pass out programs; however, a nominal greeter is no substitute for natural community care. I remember praying that the Spirit of Jesus would stir the individuals at MAC to reach out in a caring way as people mingle at the coffee bar or as parents meet each other outside the children's rooms.

The muddy shoes, compliments of a sub-par parking lot, represent a deeper MAC value. As a church, we are underfunded. We do not target college students, yet many of them seem to be drawn to MAC. This means we don't have the financial resources most churches our size do. In fact, all of our staff are bi-vocational, including myself. We consider our mission to the world more important than our personal needs. An inquiry about the mission of MAC was left out in the above e-mail—just as it is missing from the lips of most church shoppers. The exact year I received this e-mail, we planted five churches, sending out nearly 600 people from our congregation on mission to reach beyond Muncie. We prefer to plant a church or two rather than restrict outreach by accruing debt for things like a paved parking lot.

I often notice two types of people who check out churches. Some shop around for a church that best serves them. Others check out churches to seek where God would lead them; they look for a place to plug in and serve the body of Christ. Bernie and Beulah are in the latter category.

They attended MAC before Judy and I arrived. As members of a former generation, they feel God's presence as they sing hymns with an organ accompaniment. I feel God's presence with an electric lead guitar. When Judy and I were hired, electric lead guitars (with of course, bass and drums) were part of the package deal. Many people left because they didn't like this new route of worship, but Bernie and Beulah stayed. I remember when the worship band and I would meet in my office to pray before service. Bernie would faithfully come, stand beside those with an electric guitar strung across their back, and pray with us. He didn't like the music, but he wept as he prayed. He and Beulah were touched when they saw a church filled with new believers. They were moved that so many people had a sense of mission. This, of course, was fruit of the Holy Spirit, not lead guitars. Bernie once remarked to me, "Those who left missed seeing the Lord work among us." I want to respond like Bernie and Beulah when the incidentals of the church fail to meet my expectations.

Pastors As Consumers

A consumer mentality also effects how pastors or ministry leaders view the world outside the church walls. As they plan their services and ministries, it can be tempting to listen to what people in the community want in a church. Church leaders are encouraged to see what people are hungry for and then feed them that type of food. Instead of waiting upon the Holy Spirit to alert us to true needs as we live amongst the community, we choose the synthetic route and manufacture a strategy to attract people to our doors (or to keep them inside).

Ask your church this question: Do we allow the culture to filter our decisions for our churches or are we churches whom the Holy Spirit uses amongst our culture? So often the Christian church today would rather be on the cusp of what is new and exciting instead of on the cutting edge of God's handiwork. The Kingdom of God should shape a culture—not be oppressed by it. The Kingdom of God is *good* for humanity. When the Kingdom is at hand there is less sickness, corruption, and evil, and more care, selflessness, and breaking down of prejudices. Do we want the Kingdom or the best the world has to offer us today? When we research and analyze influences outside the church to determine how we inside the church should behave, we are dictated by the culture instead of by Christ. We are passing up the best for trends that are weak and fickle in comparison.

The church with a consumer mentality is like a nervous teenager who just moved to a new high school. She intently watches how the rest of the students arrive at school, how they dress, what they eat, if they eat, their attitude in class, and how they treat and talk about certain teachers. She gathers all this information and files it away so that tomorrow, she will fit in. The next morning she fine-tunes her wardrobe. She fiddles with hair and makeup. She learns a new walk. She corrects her attitude about her art appreciation class. Maybe these changes take place slowly over time and only her concerned mother notices. But over time she makes small alterations in order to be better received by her peers in this new school. This girl had such a low opinion of herself she became someone new in response to her environment. She believed she had nothing to offer her peers.

You can be sure that whatever the Lord is leading you to do in response to your love for Him and for the glory of His Kingdom, it will be relevant to where you live.

• • •

When pastors or congregations build a church by their own power, we are often left with unnecessary pain, and the beauty of the bride is only partially realized. At her core, she is still the bride and she is still chosen of God, but so much potential is left unseen.

There is an alternative. Christ wants to build His Church. He desires to display His workmanship in our churches so that we resemble Him and carry His fingerprints.

The church is His anyway.

Questions for Reflection

1. Does your church resemble a professional church, a traditional church, or a consumer-driven church? If so, how so?

2. Describe the difference between shopping for a church and being led to a church.

3. How do you respond when the incidentals of the church fail to meet your expectations?

4. Do we allow the culture to filter our decisions for our churches or are we churches whom the Holy Spirit uses amongst the culture?

For a detailed breakdown comparing the professional and traditional churches and the church God builds (as described in Chapter 4), see pages 135-138.

Chapter 4
God's Workmanship

God is actively shaping each of us. He is preparing us to carry out His purposes for the body of Christ. This is happening whether you realize it or not. Chances are, you don't know what He's up to because His preparatory work rarely unveils itself in a linear fashion. Instead, His work appears convoluted and unconnected at first glance. Years pass and experiences amass until one day you find yourself further along in life, in the midst of fulfilling something greater than yourself, too complicated to have arranged on your own. If you take the time to stop and reflect, you will see His workmanship, how all the details were perfectly arranged, and how the perceived random gave way to rational basis.

He uses our natural inclinations, our giftings, and even our mundane interests for His ministry. When we develop these interests and do the things He's put within us to do, we can positively impact the body of Christ—and by extension the world—in ways we never dreamed possible.

In my case, it all began with coffee.

I guess you could say I inherited my interest in coffee. My mom was a gourmet cook fascinated with the entire dining experience, including after-dinner drinks. Before the debut of the Krups line, she owned a stovetop cappuccino maker. Soon enough experimenting with coffee captured my interest as well, and in the early '80s, a friend gave me my first screw-top espresso machine. I'd cart it around with me and whip up drinks for friends and family since, at that time, only two espresso-based coffee shops existed in central Illinois where I lived.

Over a decade later, a friend from my hometown opened a homemade, hand-dipped ice cream store. He considered contracting with a man who supplied fair food—elephant ears and dinky donuts. I protested. "Bob, there's nothing better than ice cream and coffee. You gotta get an espresso bar!" He blew off my suggestion citing a strapped budget, but I cut him a deal. I would supply a commercial espresso machine, the beans, and the syrups while he supplied the cups, milk, and labor. We'd split the profits in the end. I made my first sale and in six months the profits paid off the machine.

At that time my pastoral salary from Muncie Alliance Church totaled $265 a week—barely enough to provide for my family. Placing espresso bars in existing businesses seemed to be a great supplemental income—especially since no one in Muncie served specialty coffee. The family business, Guido's Coffee and Espresso Equipment, started up as we placed machines in three frozen yogurt stores and one in a downtown Muncie street cart.

Next, I set my sights on a bakery in the Muncie Mall. Setting up a meeting with the manager, I pitched her the same profit-sharing plan I had set up with my friend Bob. The meeting ended with a verbal agreement. I mailed her the contract, purchased the equipment, moved it into the store, and began training employees. Within a few weeks, my instincts proved correct. The bar was a hit with shoppers and the cookie counter turned out to be our best account. With Christmas a few months away, the possibilities danced in my head.

Sometime in October the phone rang. It was the cookie lady. The conversation began friendly enough as we both mentioned how pleased we were with sales. "But we need to get this machine out of here." Her words stunned me. The constant demand for lattes kept the employees from baking cookies, she explained.

"Why can't you hire another baker?" Apparently the size of the store only allowed for one. Besides, she wasn't convinced another pair of hands would be cost-effective.

"But we have an agreement," I objected.

There was a pause.

"I didn't sign anything." I sunk. I had yet to receive a signed contract from her.

"Do you think that's right?" I tried to keep my voice calm.

"I don't really care. Just get it out of there." I suggested other adjustments that might improve the situation without ridding the store of my machine. Not buying it, she slowly lost patience with me.

"Get it out, or I'm calling the police." The force of her words ended the conversation. How would we pay for $5,000 worth of equipment while making only $13,800 a year?

I didn't care for that cookie lady.

God Will Lead Us

Unbeknownst to me, God was leading us into His will kicking and screaming. Romans 8:14 says, "...because those who are led by the Spirit of God are sons of God." Throughout the New Testament, this Greek word for "led" shows up in a variety of situations. Think of authorities bringing a criminal before a judge, an adult leading a child by the hand, a caretaker transporting the sick to the doctor. These examples occur under very different circumstances and bring to life the truth of Romans 8:14.

In the case of the accused, their hands, quite literally, are tied. A variation of the word "led" appears in Matthew 10:18 when Jesus warns the disciples they will be brought before governors and kings. In Matthew 28:46, authorities led Jesus before Pilate. The wheels of history were turning and no one possessed the power to stop it. Often those being led find themselves in circumstances that appear to be out of their control.

This word also surfaces in situations where people were plagued with inability. The people would bring their sick to Jesus just as the Good Samaritan brought the badly beaten Jew to the inn.[17] God brought Israel a Savior, and God brings glory to those with faith in Jesus.[18] In this instance, the kindness and compassion of the leader brought restoration to the needy.

In the midst of uneasiness, and perhaps against their will, people can be led. Think of the adulterous woman whom the Pharisees brought before Jesus.[19] Caught red-handed, I doubt she wanted anyone to see her, let alone a renowned rabbi. Barnabas also led someone. In Jerusalem the disciples were afraid of a Christian killer named Saul—recently going by the name of Paul—who kept showing up on their doorsteps. Barnabas ended up bridging the gap between the disciples' fear and Paul's sordid past. He physically grabbed Paul and led him to the apostles in Acts 9:27.

Jesus showed how people can be led in willing obedience. In Luke 4:1 the Spirit led Jesus into the wilderness, and He sets the example of how we are to follow the voice of God. In the Garden of Gethsemane Jesus uses this same Greek word, but it is translated "going" in English. He said, "Let us be going; the one who betrays me is at hand."[20] Jesus wasn't suggesting they run from the mob; He foretold the immediate future. Soon the mobs would deliver them over to authorities. As God, Jesus did have control over the situation, yet He complied like a sheep being led to slaughter.

We need to be led, whether against our will or in obedience.

In Romans 8:14, the leader is committed to the one being led. And this verse doesn't imply the follower chooses to be led. I assumed the worst when the cookie lady kicked my machine out of her store. But God used the actions of the confectioner to channel me, my wife Judy, and even MAC in a new direction. The Holy Spirit is committed to the ones He has sealed. We were about to walk a new line because that is what He desired for us.

No other businesses were likely candidates for the machine, so I dropped it off at MAC and started making lattes on Sunday mornings.

Soon enough, Yonder (the son of a hippie), his wife Natalie, and Deb, another student at MAC, created a music venue at the church building. I prepared my lattes while they brought in local bands. Between concerts, artists shared their work and I also made a few appearances. I shared the finer points of the coffee world in "A Coffee Moment with Papa Guido" and delivered a monologue—an analogy lifted from the word of God and spoken in a timely language—for a segment titled "The Parable." The result was a mix between a coffeehouse and a fast-moving variety show without the hokiness.

Yonder, Natalie, and Deb, proponents of community, shied away from creating another Christian hub. In addition to Christian bands, they invited others who carried a different worldview. Edgy young people started showing up at church. It wasn't unusual for the smell of pot to waft in from the parking lot during concerts. Inevitably, a few of us cleaned up beer bottles and cigarette butts outside the front door the morning after a concert. We didn't mind. The alternative crowd of the mid-'90s was attending church and hearing the word of God.

Thanks to the notoriety of the coffeehouse, opportunities presented themselves so Judy and I could pay off the equipment ejected from the mall. Taylor University asked us to cater an espresso bar for a Christmas soirée. A few months later, we were back for a Valentine's Day banquet. The need for aesthetically pleasing, portable, tabletop bars became apparent with each new catering job. So I designed and built one.

This, in turn, affected my existing business. In addition to selling espresso machines, I now began to design the counter and layout for specialty coffee equipment. Soon enough I envisioned espresso bars everywhere and even designed a portable bar to fit in the back of a van.

Each time our business diversified or reached new markets, I wondered if I was getting sidetracked. In the midst of daydreaming about the coffee business, I would ask God if I was losing my first love. For weeks at a time, I poured my emotional energy into the business.

Through circumstances and the words of people He seemed to be giving me the green light, dissolving any guilt. Like a father to a child, the reassurances made me feel as though He wanted to keep me occupied. *Go play in the corner with your coffee*, the Father seemed to be saying to His son, *and stay out of My way*.

MAC began to burst at the seams. With two services on Sundays, over 250 people jammed themselves in a room meant for 150. People arrived fifteen minutes early to claim a spot on a pew covered in burnt-orange fabric. Everyone else spilled over onto shag carpet of the same color in the aisles and out into the hallway. There were so many people packed into one place we were forced to run the air-conditioner in January and February, months when the thermometer outside boasted ten degrees below zero. On Friday nights the thriving coffeehouse ministry drew in those who wouldn't normally grace the doors of a church. With all the activity, I slowly fell behind in the demands of the church and our dismally small budget kept me from adding staff. Praying about the problem, the Lord dropped a familiar request on my heart. *Guy, I want you to start an internship program. I want you to train young people for ministry.*

• • •

During my interview for the pastor position at MAC, I mentioned I thought the church would eventually start a training program to plant other churches. This wasn't just an idea I borrowed from another successful church or pastor. Long ago God hinted where He'd eventually lead me. While living with twenty-eight other guys at a Bible institute, I remember being astounded by their passion to preach the Gospel. I remember climbing up into my bunk bed, wondering if I could ever exude that sort of passion, if God would ever call me to something exciting. He stirred my heart with His plans for my future and I believed He could use me just as He planned to use them. *You'll raise up and train young people for ministry.* I tucked my destiny away in my heart. Seven years later, the promise unfolded when I oversaw an internship at my first church, the Lilly Chapel School of Ministry. We trained students in doctrine and offered practical ministry experience with the intent to plant churches. Was God asking me to do the same at MAC?

When God unearthed His familiar request, I had been asking Him for help around the church. I assumed He planned to provide me that help through the students we would train. I began to think through the logistics. At the School of Ministry, students paid tuition. I didn't feel right asking future interns to pay tuition in order to help me run errands or clean the church. Perhaps they could raise support just as the university ministry leaders I knew did before reporting to campus. The downside was they had to leave campus when their support fell below a certain percentage. This wasn't a great solution either.

But God had not made a request without providing a way to accomplish it. Once again, He had been faithful to arrange all the elements necessary to bring about His plan. We are His sons and daughters, and He had been leading us by His Spirit whether we realized it or not.

Nearly a decade before I stepped foot in Muncie, Indiana, Judy and I had visited our friends Chris and Nancy in Bloomington, Minnesota. Students at the Bethany College of Missions, they attended tuition free as they trained to be missionaries. Their schedule included classes from eight to noon, and in the afternoons they worked around campus or for one of Bethany's entrepreneurial ventures. The students' afternoon jobs offset the costs of the college's overhead and upkeep.

Perhaps this model would work for the MAC internship. By now, my business had set up over thirty coffeehouses and all needed a place to buy coffee beans. I had directed them to a roaster in Chicago. But if MAC owned a coffee roaster, the interns could learn about ministry in the morning and roast beans to support themselves in the afternoon.

I sensed God was allowing something to click into place. I prayed, not a prayer from a testing heart, but one from a deep place of understanding. "Okay God. I'm not going to do this unless You come through. What I have to strive to start, I'm going to have to strive to maintain. If You want this thing, You'll make it happen. I'm asking You for two confirmations: a coffee roaster so the interns can be paid while they are serving and learning, and a house for them to live in rent-free." His ultimate plan was distant and not yet defined, but I knew my prayer lined up with His heart.

Because I knew God wanted it, I was tempted to produce it. He could use me to bring about His will, to help Him along. Maybe I am to put "legs on my prayers," as they say. Not sure how we'd pull it off, I thought Judy and I could buy a roaster and then hire the interns ourselves.

Tough to convince, Judy questioned the wisdom of blurring the church's finances with our own. Also, she didn't want the responsibility of the interns' income resting on Guido's Coffee. But I desperately wanted to do an internship program. I kept trying to convince her with new proposals.

The Christmas Gift

Shortly thereafter, a man walked into the church and knocked on my office door. He introduced himself and mentioned we shared a mutual friend. As he sat down, he explained his wife had read a feature in *Reader's Digest* about a family who decided to do away with the accepted Christmas traditions one year. In the place of their own gift exchange, they purchased new safety equipment for a local hockey team who couldn't afford the regulation gear. He explained to me how the article had generated an idea for his wife's perfect Christmas gift: She could become a benefactor of ministry. Taking initiative, he was secretly interviewing ministries in the area to surprise her on Christmas morning.

I was sitting in a rare meeting. This man was asking me where he could spend his money in our church.

I expressed MAC had a few current needs based on our expectation of where God was leading us. Not knowing how generous Christmas gift exchanges were at this man's house, I took a deep breath and started with my most outlandish request: a coffee roaster. I explained how we hoped to support interns with a coffee roasting company while they trained for ministry. Thinking my first request might carry too hefty of a price tag, I mentioned another. "We're also looking to buy an espresso machine for a coffee cart in the Ball State dorms. We'd like to offer complimentary lattes and mochas to the students for late night study breaks. An espresso machine costs anywhere from $3,000 to $8,000," I added, watching him closely to gauge his reaction. As we were willing to receive anything he was willing to give, I ended our meeting with a request for a coffee grinder for the church.

Later that afternoon I received a call at the church.

"Is this the coffee church?" the woman asked.

"Some people say that," I chuckled. "What can we do for you?"

"Do you have a coffee club? The reason I ask is, I'm interested in purchasing a coffee club membership for my brother-in-law for Christmas."

"I'm sorry," I answered. We don't have a coffee club. But call us next year—we're praying for a roaster."

As God would have it, I would cross the path of the mystery caller again. Neither of us knew this at the time of the call but she was the wife who had read the *Reader's Digest* article and I had just met with her husband! In a few short weeks, she would provide the means for us to begin a coffee-of-the-month club—she just didn't know it yet.

Within the week, her husband returned to MAC and handed over a check. "I want you to buy a coffee roaster." I took a glance. The boxed-in number was larger than my current annual salary.

"There are only two conditions." I stiffened as I feared the dream was slipping away, marred by a large plaque on the wall, stock options in our baby company, or a seat on the executive committee that didn't yet exist. Not interested in the strings I assumed he would connect to this check, I prepared to list other places he could give his money.

He replied, "I want to remain anonymous…and do you think you could drop off a pound of coffee every so often?"

• • •

"Fred! We're in the coffee business!" I exclaimed to our district superintendent moments after the man left the church.

The prospect of an entrepreneurial venture in the church surprised him. "Normally we don't link a business directly into the church," Fred replied. "I'm concerned for a few reasons: It's not our policy, we don't have any precedent for this, and more importantly, it could be an issue with the IRS."

I explained to him how the training internship had been a long-standing call in my life, how the idea to fuse business and ministry came about, how I felt my specific prayer had been the heart of God, and how a man dropped by my office one day and bought us a roaster. He recognized God's hand at work and sensed His leading to break precedent and tradition. He and Jon, another district leader, helped us navigate through IRS issues and policy matters in the denominational district office. Finally, Alliance World Coffees (AWC), MAC's first mission-supporting business became a reality.

After making progress in the district office, Fred and Jon made a trip to Muncie. Sitting in a circle drinking coffee, Fred sat back and began the meeting with, "Now tell me, Guy, what's your vision for this church?" I described how we slowly bumbled along, staying true to what God had written across our hearts until the coffee roaster and subsequent internship program came about. In hindsight, this was all too perfect, too well organized. This wasn't my vision; I hadn't been the one to think up the master plan. God was arranging people and circumstances.

"So what can we do to help?" Fred asked.

At the spur of the moment I blurted out, "What about buying us an intern house?"

The story of God's hand creating something new at MAC traveled through the district office and eventually reached the desk of Donald, the district treasurer. The following May when the Annual Council met, I told the District Leadership Team that a house with great specifications was on the market in Muncie. Immediately, Donald acted. Back in 1996, the district sold Dr. A. W. Tozer's church in Oaklawn, Illinois, and some money from the sale remained unallocated. Donald wanted to use the funds to purchase a house for the MAC interns. During a break at the council meeting, he viewed the house online and made an offer. In the end, the Leadership Team favored his decision and by June, they purchased the house. We named it the Tozer House.

God wants it more than we do.

• • •

God is always arranging circumstances and people in His church. At MAC, we expected Him to lead us and then we followed Him down an unconventional path. It wasn't always clean or easy. AWC failed financially for the first two years—our debt topped $15,000. Our first attempt at branding Vecino's Coffee also failed. But He knows where we are going, even when we don't. If we follow God—the one who knows the purposes He has written across the hearts of His people—we will display His workmanship. His workmanship always creates something that suggests divine intervention. We can become churches that weren't planned and witness the personal nature of our God.

Questions for Reflection

1. How has God led you or your church against your will?

2. What is the difference between forecasting future ministries in the church and driving a five-year plan?

CHAPTER 5

OPEN THE DOOR

Ironically, when a church feels secure and settled, they may be on their way to spiritual weakness. When accumulated wealth buys spacious facilities filled with able staff and high-tech gadgets, when budgets are comfortably in the black, and when the attendance becomes the envy of surrounding churches, a church finds herself in a dangerous position. Drastic measures might be in order to ward off spiritual stagnation. If they are satisfied with how they look and how others perceive them, and if self-sufficiency solves every challenge, the spiritual slump has already begun.

The Laodicean church described in Revelations 3:14-22 was secure and settled. Much like the church listed above, they were never in enough trouble to be thrown a rope, let alone be at the end of it. Their self-reliance always provided options to remedy any glitch before it swelled into a full-blown crisis. The church of Laodicea appeared strong to men, an example of autonomy meant to be emulated. But as they rolled merrily along, Jesus stood on the outside of His church. He wanted to be admitted inside—He was knocking on their door—but they couldn't hear Him. What a frighting picture: a church believing they are on the right track when Jesus can't be found within the church walls.

Christ's rebuke reveals the reality of the Laodicean church lurking beneath her candy shell. "You say, 'I am rich, and have become wealthy, and have need of nothing,' and you do not know that you are wretched and miserable and poor and blind and naked."[21] Impressive wealth and status masked spiritual poverty and nakedness. God's mission got lost in the shuffle as they focused on meeting their own needs. Christ's reprimand was due to the Laodiceans continually choosing the safe over the risky, added to their lack of passion, sacrifice, and a sense of call. The gleaming report card turned out to be a bunch of smoke and mirrors. The body in Laodicea was stagnant, stale, and lukewarm.

This type of spiritual climate in the church feels *physically* uncomfortable to Jesus. The mind-numbing lack of empathy and joy, the security of always knowing how to proceed, the recycled annual plans—I think they set Christ's nerves on edge. He can't stand to see programming and precedent prop up weak ministries. In a Laodicean church He needs to escape much like we do when confronted with uncomfortable situations. Haven't you ever wished you could melt through the floorboards when sharing a room with a parent dealing with a tantrum-throwing child? What about the last time when you had dinner with a couple who fought passively aggressively with cutting humor and awkward remarks? I bet you couldn't wait for the check. When Jesus' discomfort in the Laodicean church finally peaked, He walked out. Instead of sticking around and enduring the agony, He soundlessly walked out into the night in need of some fresh air.

The story would be pretty depressing if it ended there. Thankfully, it doesn't. When He left the church, He didn't leave the city or the block. He couldn't even get past the curb. He loitered out on the sidewalk for a few minutes, breathing deeply and running His hands through His hair, trying to calm down. Eventually, because of His grace and love, He turned around to face that front door. His heart propelled His hand and He began to knock. He gave them a second chance. Here was their opportunity to open up their ears, to listen, to notice their loss, and to welcome Him back in so He could build His church His way.

When We Hear Him Knocking

MAC once received this second chance. Both the congregation and I had made a grab for the reigns of the church, hoping to steer her toward our own ideals. For two years I had been a professional pastor driving the activities of the church. By my plans, I attempted to drum up some spiritual excitement in the church body. Judy and I tried every strategy that had worked for us in the past, but nothing changed for the better. The congregation's traditional mentality harmed the livelihood of the church body as well. Accustomed to running the affairs of the church for years, maybe even decades before Judy and I entered the scene, they felt threatened by our initiatives. All this to say, with the pastor and congregation fighting for control, Jesus had slipped out the front door of MAC at some point.

Both the congregation and I were acting out of self-sufficiency, and our ideas and plans were wildly at odds. We eventually crashed, as you saw in a previous chapter; once the dust settled, the church body had taken a hit. We had decreased by sixty percent and so had our budget. Those of us left took drastic measures to stay afloat. We sold everything in the church that wasn't nailed down. We were still unable to make our mortgage payments on the church building, so the district paid off our loan and suspended our payments. When these measures didn't balance the budget, Judy and I volunteered to take a pay cut.

And the bad news kept arriving. It was during this hamstrung state of the church that our riding lawn mower died. It happened while a member of our congregation cut the lawn around the swing set. Unbeknownst to him, he caught one of the swings under the front of the mower. Before he could respond, as the machine chugged forward, the swing stubbornly remained hooked beneath, hoisting up the front end until it stood vertical. The driver scrambled out of the way as the lawn mower crashed down, wheels spinning in the air. The motor kept running as the oil drained out of the engine, which in turn starved the crank shaft and cylinder. In layman's terms, the engine burnt up, damaged beyond repair. To make matters worse, the mower died during the time of year when Indiana lawns need a cut every five days or so. We didn't have the spare cash to purchase a replacement. This meant that in two weeks, the church property would look like an abandoned lot.

We planned to discuss the cash flow problem during our next congregational meeting—but the Holy Spirit showed up. Of all the places in time and space where He could have been, He chose to show up in a meeting about a lawn mower. Once everyone had gathered, Bernie, the eldest member in the church, preempted the discussion. Noticeably moved by the Spirit, he stood up and said, "We're not going to figure this out like a business. This is God's church; this is His problem. Let's go to the front to pray." Bernie heard knocking. Our pathetic little problem had opened his ears so he could hear. And then, that's when it happened. He opened the door of the church for us and welcomed Christ back in.

As we walked to the front of the church together and knelt in prayer, we corporately owned an important foundational principle: The church is God's. He will build His church and provide for her as He has faithfully done throughout the centuries. This act of opening the door happened during a simple choice to seek God's solutions, but coming to this point had been a two-year process. The spider web, the stacked deck, the major exodus, Judy and I coming to the end of our rope as leaders—all this laid the groundwork for this decision, this breaking point. The situation, as simple and mundane as it was, had become spiritually critical. In desperation, we needed God to show up. We heard knocking, opened the door, and Jesus entered, eclipsing two damaging mentalities in MAC. He broke down my CEO pastor mentality and the traditional church mentality of the congregation. The old ways of running a church died when the truth of Christ's headship settled into our hearts. On that hot summer day, by our decision to pray about a dead mower, we allowed God to solve our problem. We opened the door and crowned Jesus as head of His church.

Other Humble Entrances

We might not notice the faint knocking with all the other noises in our churches, but isn't it interesting how quickly a problem can capture all our senses? Trouble creates resistance, gumming up and clogging the natural flow and order of things. Like poking a stick through the spokes of a moving bike, predicaments can send us sprawling. But with our faces in the dirt, our ears perk up, we look around for answers, and we begin to realize we might need some help. When messes and problems arrive in our churches, we have an opportunity to open the door to Jesus. We can choose to invite Him back in to lead us to His solutions, or we can choose to skirt the situation and find a self-sufficient answer—to get back on the bike, so to speak, and ride off on the same course as if nothing just happened.

A friend called me during one such trial in his church. A sixteen-year-old girl in his congregation became pregnant. Astonished, the congregation wondered what would happen next—how would they deal with this failing in their midst? Most weren't expecting my friend's response. "We're going to give her a shower and help her raise the child."

"But if we give her a shower, aren't we condoning premarital sex?"

Here we have an example of the Lord knocking on the door of His church hidden in a difficult, messy situation. Will the church welcome Him in?

What about those with mild handicaps who create disturbances during the sermon? What happens when a pastor unveils his ten-year affair or when an addict relapses? What happens when a church can't pay the mortgage or when a congregation insists on fighting?

These issues often bring resistance to the everyday workings of a church. We can choose to deal with these "problems" as swiftly and quietly as possible or we can choose to view them as an opportunity to foster a welcoming environment for Jesus.

How We Bar the Door

So often the church botches the opportunity to make Christ feel at ease in its midst due to precautionary measures. A timely crisis that needs immediate action is strangled to death by red tape.

For instance, a few single moms at one church began contacting Joe, a mechanic, with questions about car maintenance. Their needs ranged from simple oil changes to a second opinion on the whining noise coming from the engine. He helped them out, free of charge, and guessed there might be other single moms in the same predicament. Thinking this would be a great way for the church to minister, he gathered a few other mechanics and planned to offer free car service on the first Saturday of each month to those with a need. What an easy ministry to start up, right? Not necessarily.

The church has become too bulky and bureaucratic to welcome Jesus into its midst in a timely fashion. Jesus is outside the door and we hear Him knocking, but we need three committees to open the door: the grounds committee, the finance committee, and the committee for committees!

Cut through the red tape. Dismiss the parliamentary procedure. Forgo the government to meet a need. Layers of government in our churches have too long been acceptable. They have been passed down to the detriment of future generations. Now it is too easy to fall into the roles of the priest and the Levite in Jesus's Good Samaritan illustration. It is nearly impossible to stop and immediately help those in need. We're too busy doing committee work. Over and over Jesus is getting passed by because we're rushing off to board meetings.

Tolerating the Messy

Just as bulky bureaucracies keep Christ at bay in His church, so does the act of guarding the church to keep her holy. Remember the predicament in my friend's church and the response of some to throwing a shower for an unwed teenager? "Won't we be condoning premarital sex?" To throw a party for *that*, and *in the church* no less, we feel as though we're defiling the church. Furthermore, following the advice of the pastor would seem to invite additional problems and additional stains upon the bride's white garment. It's a difficult choice to embrace something messy given our propensities toward the neat, the clean, and the orderly.

During the height of the Jesus Movement, hippies began showing up in churches across the nation. Not too long after, signs appeared in the entrances of churches, requiring shoes be worn during the services.

The church exerts great effort toward keeping herself tidy and clean, both physically and spiritually. By picking up the rough kids and bringing them to youth group or by opening up a soup kitchen after a costly renovation, we're inviting disorder. We're inviting mess and headaches. And there's a chance the church might project an image that's little less than perfect, and actually a little haphazard.

So often what we're not comfortable with makes Jesus feels right at home. Throughout the Gospels, Jesus engaged with the world. He touched the lepers, spoke to the prostitutes, and ate with the swindlers. He didn't refuse them and He didn't separate Himself because the less-than-perfect could not overcome His purity. As believers, we are one with this same Christ. Nothing in the world can rob us of our grace-given purity. In other words, "the called-out ones" and "the separated" are terms and phrases that describe what we *already are* as Christians. To be holy and set apart is our identity—not actions we must take in order to be pure. Mixing with a spiritually mixed crowd will not change who we are in Christ.

Tolerating the Unplanned

Sometimes good ideas and watertight plans jostle Christ out of His place as head of the church and push Him toward the back until the only space left for Him to stand is out on the front stoop. Church experts teach us to write up a church vision statement and plaster it to the opposite wall in our office. We then proceed to filter each agenda item or ministry idea that crosses our desk through the vision statement hanging before us. Maybe some of us don't have a formal mission statement, but in our hearts of hearts we know what we want for our churches.

In the '90s when I arrived at Muncie, I had my heart set on leading a church focused on the baby boomers. This generation appealed to me because the experts kept touting their size and openness to try new things as great assets for growing large, relevant churches. If I targeted this group, I'd have the best shot of leading a large church and I was convinced the contemporary style of music and dress—the ways of worshiping that I was comfortable with—would appeal to this generation. Besides, the baby boomers were the hip target group during the late '80s and early '90s, and I wanted to be hip like everyone else. But the baby boomers in Muncie weren't pleased with my casual approach to church and college students kept showing up at our door. This was a problem. All the seminars and conferences warned me about this cohort. They are a drag on ministry for two specific reasons: high turnover rates and low financial assets.

College students didn't fit into my context of ministry. But Christ was steering our church in a new direction through the likes of people He brought to our door. At some point we had to decide whether or not our mission statements, ideas, hopes, and dreams for the church would accept Christ's purposes for His church.

Christ doesn't always barge into our churches. He gently raps at our front doors. We are free to fulfill our five-year plan by targeting and strategizing for specific groups, regardless of whoever shows up, or by strategizing for specific ministries we want our church to have. We're free to keep pushing in one direction while Christ offers another.

I don't have a five-year plan, but when people ask, I can give them highlights as to where I *think* we might be going. For instance, based on the way God has stacked the deck here at MAC, someday we might be training young people for ministry based out of a youth hostel in Europe, financially supported through an international business. When I picture this in my mind, play it out, and dream about it, it's easy to align people and resources in that direction. But it is also easy for me to have tunnel vision. Instead, I need to hold these dreams loosely. I need to leave space for the unexpected, making allowances for twist and turns stirred by the Spirit. If I focus singularly on a youth hostel in Europe and excuse the other opportunities Christ brings to His church—a stirred layperson with a heart for ministry elsewhere, a messy dilemma, a moment of desperation—I begin to run the church in a rectilinear fashion. In other words, I believe I need to move in a straight line where success of the goal depends upon speed and velocity. If I'm not careful with my thoughts about the future of the church, I begin depending upon calculations and mathematics for achievement in the church. Churches will be better off if we leave space for the wild side and the mystery, for side trips and scenic views. Jesus has a mind of His own, yet we often only give Him ours to work with.

The sad truth is that Jesus will go around the church if we don't open the door to Him. He'll hang out with the stirred laypeople, the ones barred from acting in the church because of red tape, precaution, or stringent five-year plans. It's no problem for Him to follow them home and build a ministry there—a para-church ministry. Jesus will always move toward hurting people. We in the church will miss out on His presence and His ministry if we refuse to open the door to Him. God's presence is always with His mission.

Gold Refined by Fire

We have become conditioned by our churchy systems. Whether we are a part of a traditional or professional church, or have a consumer mentality, our ability to open the door to Christ is compromised by these frameworks. We act a lot like the children of Israel who, having been slaves, continued to think like slaves even after they received freedom. "Life was easier back there," they reminisced. "The rules were clear. We knew what we were supposed to do and what was expected of us." Returning to the familiar frameworks and ignoring questions and uncertainty in exchange for a smoother journey is a sure way to end up in lukewarm waters.

In response to the Laodicean church, a church treading in lukewarm waters, Jesus said, "I advise you to buy from Me gold refined by fire so that you may become rich..."[22] Gold is found when God sends radicals and misfits to shape the church and we give them a voice despite our prejudices. Gold shows up when we hang out with the adultrous father who just destroyed his marriage. A Laodicean church buys gold when they destroy their self-sufficiency, the red tape, their perfectionism, and their five-year plans—all remnants of the Babylonian culture. Let go of these flimsy candy-shells and let God build something with gold.

Choosing to wipe out layers of government, to get involved in the messes, and to flush the calculated plans are difficult choices to make. Following through with them will take acts of passion. In consolation, Jesus will be there with you. He would rather spend time with those passionately following Him than the listless, floating wherever the strongest current takes them.

These choices are difficult, but formative. When a church reaches a breaking point and invites Jesus back into her midst, they have cleared away the human paradigms. They have torn down the old building, so to speak, and laid a new foundation. Jesus is now free to uniquely build the church.

Think back to the church with the teenage pregnancy. By opening the door to Jesus and embracing this young mother, the church lays a foundation of mercy. Furthermore, they open the door for others who need mercy—as Jesus returns to His church, many others often enter in His wake. Suddenly, by one decision, through one breaking point, the church begins to look different. They aren't what they once were. Jesus is shaping them in new ways. They reflect Him more clearly. And the best part about this scenario is that it wasn't about something the church started or dreamed up. It was about what Jesus had brought to them and how they responded to it. Wouldn't you want to hand down this legacy to future generations over the alternative—how to construct mission statements, five-year plans, or lessons on how to keep a church tidy and running like a well-oiled machine?

Sometimes when we open the door to Jesus, God moves us into circumstances out of our control. In those times He will meet us in His power and surprise us as we determine not to rely upon man's wisdom and strategies. Remember, the Babylonian culture robs us of what God has prepared for us. It rips us off of living in the midst of God's creativity. When we invite Him in, we trade man's solutions and designs for His creativity. If we open the door to Christ and allow Him to build His Church, we will go places we've never dreamed. Then, someday down the road, we'll have a moment to look back over the years. As we catch up with God's perspective, we'll marvel at His creativity and His meticulous preparation.

Questions for Reflection

1. How have we pushed Christ out of His church?

2. Where do you hear Christ knocking at the door of your church?

3. What kind of people does your church community avoid?

Chapter 6

Avoid Ishmaels

Before long, anyone visiting MAC will hear: "God wants it more than we do." We've repeated the phrase enough, it has become our family's shorthand—a simplistic quip that carries a backlog of stories long enough to last a patient listener through two lattes. If you've been a patient reader, I've shared most of these stories with you already.

But in addition to the stories, the phrase is an abridged version of the principles guiding our approach to ministry. Our shorthand represents *chazon*-vision. God will reveal His plans for building His church. He has purposes for us and when the time is right He will make them happen by moving the hearts of people to attend to what He reveals. We repeat our phrase to remind us of this truth in times when we're tempted to build the church ourselves—when we need our faith bolstered because it appears as though God has forgotten about us.

The *it* in our phrase is dense with meaning as well. For starters, this modest pronoun encompasses all the general commands and promises God has already spelled out in His word. To name a few, He wants people to be saved from their sins and trained in the knowledge of Christ. He wants to provide for the physical, emotional, and spiritual needs plaguing humanity. He wants His glory to be displayed. God wants these things more than we do. But in addition to our general purposes, God also has specific purposes and promises in mind for each of us. God writes holy desires upon our hearts. He calls and stirs us to a mission that gives purpose to our lives. Abraham would become the father of a great nation. Moses would free his brothers from Pharoah's tyranny. Paul would be the apostle to the Gentiles. He wants His children to fulfill their purposes more than we want to fulfill them.

Waiting for God

Believing God wants it more than we do directly affects the actions of our churches, despite those who find our expression resigned or passive. As Christ reveals His plans for the body, we'll be tempted to adopt what God has unveiled and to start off in the flesh. First, we must actively wait for God's timing.

When God promised to stack the deck, He said He would bring in the right people at the right time to do the right things to build His church. With this promise in hand, I could have forged ahead without Him. For instance, I could have prepared for the promise by building a church auditorium large enough to hold all the people He promised to bring—justifying my actions by claiming I had taken God at His word. Instead, I waited on God and it was a good thing I did. By "stacking the deck," God meant He would add to us, but the promise also meant we would be giving away people to do the work of the Kingdom elsewhere. Since the stacked-deck encounter, counting all the church sites, we are about 2,000 people strong, but we have never needed to seat over 800 people in Muncie. Building an auditorium to seat thousands would have been a big mistake.

When we see God's purposes for our future, we find ourselves at a crossroads. We can wait for God to organically move His church forward into those purposes, or we can run ahead and force these purposes through human means. In other words, we can move forward in the energy of the Spirit or in the energy of the flesh. In the early '90s, God asked me to start a ministry training program at MAC. I desperately wanted this and planned to fund this training program myself with my new coffee and espresso equipment business. Yet learning how "God wants it more than we do" through the stacked deck and spider web encounters, I knew I wanted this purpose to be birthed of the Spirit and not of my own initiatives. I let go of my own plans and waited for God to naturally move His church into her purpose. I placed two obstacles in front of God's request—a test for God to show He wanted the internship program more than I did. The first was a coffee roaster so the interns could financially support themselves through a coffee roasting business. The second was an intern house where they could live rent-free. When He provided the roaster and the house, we moved forward, convinced of His desires for the training program and caught up in the movement of what the Spirit had started.

When I have a legitimate call from God, such as the internship, I hate waiting. I feel as though I've been given this enormous Roman candle and a lighted match, but I can't touch flame to fuse. Staring at the objects in my hands, I want to see a beautiful explosion of color *right now*, forgetting, of course, that I am actually a piece of a much larger and more spectacular display. If I move forward without my cue, in the end I am left with less and the rest of the show is slightly weakened. Waiting has been a troublesome discpline from the start. Even Abraham, the father of our faith, faltered from time to time.

Abraham's Impatience

In Genesis 12:1-3, God promised Abraham that if he left his father's house and traveled to a new land, then God would make him the father of a great nation who would in turn bless the rest of the world. At the time of the promise, Abraham was seventy five years old and his wife Sarah was barren. Despite the obvious unliklihood of the promise, Abraham believed God, packed up, and left town.

However, in the waning years of the decade since God first spoke, Abraham began to second-guess what he had heard. Maybe God had spoken figuratively, he speculated as he sized up his current childless reality against the promise. Perhaps Abraham wouldn't actually have a son from his own body. Looking to solutions in the customs of his time, he wondered if he should adopt his chief servant, Eliezer, to carry on his line.

But back in Haran, God had spoken matter-of-factly. To impress his literal promise upon Abraham's heart once again, God called Abraham outside of his tent and drew his attention to the stars, challenging him to count them. "So shall your descendants be," He promised. Abraham believed God, and the readers of the story find out his faith was reckoned to him as righteousness.[23]

God continued His point and reminded Abraham that He was the one who brought him out of Ur of the Chaldeans and that he would inherit the land he was standing upon. "O Lord GOD, how may I know that I will possess it?" he asked in response.[24]

God instructed Abraham to prepare for a covenant agreement—God was about to back up His words with a binding promise. Abraham arranged all the necessary elements for a covenant agreement and then waited for the Lord to show up and, in effect, sign the contract. He waited. The day wore on and he kept waiting. Dusk arrived and the fatigued Abraham fell asleep. The Lord chose this moment, when Abraham was sleeping, to show up and cut a covenant with Abraham, saying, "To your descendants I have given this land…"[25]

This holy contract should have been all the assurance Abraham needed that the promises of God would come to pass just as He said they would. He experienced what many of us don't: obvious, audible words from the very mouth of the God. To make matters even easier for Abraham, the Lord completed the covenant without him—while he was sleeping. This meant Abraham had nothing to do, no conditions to fill in order for the Lord to carry out His part of the agreement. God was the one who would make it happen. All Abraham had to do was wait on His perfect timing.

Yet after these wonderful moments of righteousness and experiencing covenant with God, Abraham became impatient and helped God along. His desperation for a son overshadowed his faith. The womb of Sarah's handmaiden, Hagar, bore Abraham his first son. This was not God's original plan. So instead of this son being the much anticipated heir of a great nation, the life and legacy of the boy named Ishmael would be racked with discord. An angel of the Lord foretold Hagar that his hand would be against everyone and everyone's hand would be against his. Ishmael grew up and lived to the east of his brothers. Fighting and hardships between Israel and her neighbors have existed even until today.[26]

Abraham became anxious and helped God fulfill His promise to him. He relied upon human solutions to solve his current problem. As a result, disaster stood in place of divine promise. Countless heartaches and tragedies could have been bypassed if Abraham and Sarah would have waited on the Lord.

What fallouts, hardships, and wounds could the church dodge if we waited on the Lord to fulfill His promises to us? How many Ishmael's have we borne?

Relaxed Concern

As we wait for God to prove He wants it more than we do, we must also practice "relaxed concern."[27] This discipline introduces some important tension to our role in the church. When you see a great need in the church or when you have a fresh sense of call, don't assume you must immediately create a ministry. Hold your calls and concerns loosely. Remember them and watch for God to move, but do not let these stirrings fall by the wayside.

Once while attending a conference, someone's testimony convicted me about my ambivalence toward the poor. As I reflected on my attitudes and lack of action, the Spirit moved me to repentance. There are many in the community of Muncie who are in need, and I wanted to adjust my behavior to be more Christ-like. In the days following the conference however, I didn't run out and try to create a ministry for the poverty-stricken. I could have jumped in headfirst, rallied the troops by preaching on the poor, cited statistics of Muncie's underprivileged, and conjured up enough guilt to motivate a few people in the congregation to start up a ministry. Pastors and congregants can get religious in these situations. We hide behind religious terminology and Bible verses; we can wrap up anything in rhetoric to make it sound like God is urgently backing up our stance. But a need does not constitute a call. Instead, I invited God to come into the church and to start working in this area. I knew He loved the poor more than me; He wants to provide for their needs more than I do.

My delay in creating a ministry did not mean I was indifferent to the poor. I chose to rest in my state of concern, believing I didn't need to strive to meet this need because it was already on the heart of God to do so. I wanted God to lead us into meeting this need as He displayed His unique purposes for the church. Practicing relaxed concern in the time following the conference, I watched, waited, paid attention, and prayed that God would move all the necessary pieces of a ministry into place.

Waiting and relaxed concern are both tied to the fact that God wants it more than we do. The absence of these disciplines in our churches sets us up for disaster. When we force promises and callings into being by our own strength, or drive a program despite a lack of genuine excitement and movement, we crowd out God. Our ministries will not display God's fingerprints, but our own. Others won't be able to look at the goings-on in our churches and witness His unique workmanship. Jesus is all powerful and "is able to do far more abundantly beyond all that we ask or think," and we can wait for Him to act.[28] We can move forward in the energy of the Spirit by paying attention and watching, expecting God to raise up what is necessary to build His church.

One word of caution: Waiting and practicing relaxed concern does not give us the leeway to lazily sit back and expect ministries and calls to work themselves out without us. When you are sure God is moving, don't let anything get in the way. In the excitement of seeing God provide all the money to purchase a roaster, I immediately sent it all off with an order for a roaster to a company up in Canada. Suffice it to say, once they had our money, they were in no hurry to ship the roaster. Months later the roaster idly sat 3,000 miles away while interns showed up at our door needing a means of financial support, and fresh accounts for locally roasted coffee piled up in our office. A man in Canada was holding up the whole operation. "Come on Josh," I said to one of the interns. "Tomorrow morning you and I are getting in a car and driving to Canada to get that roaster. We're camping out on his doorstep until he ships it." Some cautioned us to sit still, thinking we were about to create an Ishmael—that we weren't displaying relaxed concern. Not in this case. Everything necessary for this ministry was poised and ready. At this point waiting was equivalent to wasting time.

The Practicalities of Testing for the Flesh

As I've mentioned before, MAC values a grassroots approach to ministry. We're open to God moving us to do whatever, whenever, by whomever. This sets us up for lots of mess, as you might imagine. What happens when we've done the waiting, we've practiced the relaxed concern, and now five different people have spoken up with five different ideas after being stirred by the Spirit? Where do you start? There must be something in place to restrain us from running off ill-prepared. There are ways to think, make decisions, and plan without borrowing from the culture of Babylon.

At MAC we keep it simple—we keep the organizational structure to a minimum so that if God is moving, we can move quickly with Him. When someone comes to us with a sense of calling or stirring to begin a ministry, we encourage him or her to fill out a simple form with a few general questions, such as the following:

1. Please describe the ministry.
2. Why do you feel called to start this new ministry?
3. What will it take to get this ministry up and running?

4. How many people will you need to build a team and/or how many are already interested?
5. What kind of facility will you need?
6. Summarize the financial needs of this ministry.

First off, the general function of this ministry form is for the benefit of the one interested in starting a ministry rather than for any committee or leadership head. Filling out the form helps an individual clarify the good idea in his or her own mind and grapple with the real-world concerns. We ask him to weigh these issues before the Lord through prayer so he can begin to understand the considerations and parameters of his stirring. The form is NOT a springboard for crafting a plan.

We give each idea serious consideration; God might be revealing a new course for the church through this simple form. However, from time to time, we run across some ideas with obvious problems. This introduces another function of the form. Filling out this simple piece of paper helps leadership screen for obvious red flags. Reasons for dismissing a new ministry idea normally fall within three categories: incorrect theological positions, an excessive use of funds, or the questionable character of the person submitting the form.

Red Flags

One reason to snuff out a new ministry idea might be due to extreme theological views. Let's say someone feels called to start a ministry to the sick. Upon pressing this person's good idea, we begin to understand his incorrect position on healing. He believes a person needs to confess his sins and then claim God will heal him. If the sick correctly follow this procedure, then God is obligated to restore them back to health. In cases like this, someone in leadership will meet with this person, explain MAC's differing theological view, and explain why we cannot move forward into this ministry for theological reasons.

Money also factors into our screening process. If a stirred individual believes her ministry could start up with less than $1,000, and there aren't incorrect theological positions or issues of questionable character to consider, we give her the automatic go-ahead. Anything above $1,000 we don't immediately axe, but tread forward more carefully. We attempt to balance God's ability to provide for any financial need while remembering the other financial obligations within the church. We need to consider the cost of this new idea if it could potentially drain resources from other places in the church, yet realize the Lord might be leading us to trim up our expenditures anyway.

Finally, we need to check the character of the person. MAC considers the *character* of a person, not their resume and qualifications (a screening point in the professional church) or their last name, spotless past, and generous tithing (often a screening point in the traditional church). If someone is high-maintenance, hypocritical, and complains about the church, we rarely give them serious consideration. Additionally, we easily dismiss those who are not involved in the current missions of the church or are critical of them and distract others with their criticisms. On a more positive note, if the stirred individual is authentic and possesses a realistic view of himself, we're all ears. Additionally, I like to see how others in the church respond to this stirred person and his idea. If I can find people who speak highly of him and would even be open to following this person and this idea, then there is usually nothing, character-wise, stopping us from seeing where this idea might lead next.

Once someone fills out the form and passes our simple screening processes, the exercise of clarifying the good idea and grappling with real-world concerns now becomes a practical way to test for the flesh. As the church moves forward into this ministry, we test whether or not it has been birthed by the Spirit by whether or not the necessary factors of the ministry are met (such as a roaster and a house, in the case of my training program). If the parameters the stirred individual laid out are unmet, we ask them to wait and practice relaxed concern. Halting the ministry at this point doesn't necessarily mean the person missed God or didn't hear Him correctly. Timing might be the simple issue. There may be other aspects to the ministry yet to be revealed. We don't know the reason why sound Bible-based ministries don't click into place sometimes, but we ask individuals to hold this stirring loosely, waiting for God's timing and not forcing a false start.

Gathering Other Stirred Individuals

I have discovered that when God desires to do something within a church, more than one person will hear His prompts. When a ministry idea clears the "red flag screening," we introduce the person and her idea before the congregation. This action serves several functions. First, it opens up the possibility to confirm stirrings. Making an announcement tests to see if the idea is something God has written on the hearts of others in His church. If others are hearing the same message, this is something to take seriously. Secondly, an announcement rallies those who are not leaders, but share the same stirring. This brings up an important point about the various types of people God gathers in His church.

Normally the stirred individual who has taken the time to fill out our simple ministry form is the one whom I call a trigger person. This type of person normally has an entrepreneurial spirit and is a dreamer with an ever-present arsenal of big ideas. Typically, a trigger person can articulate her ideas and rally others around that idea. If God is stirring this individual with His plans, there is a possibility He has already placed this burden on the hearts of others within the church.

There will normally be some stirred organizers in the congregation. These people have the ability to see all the details of the big idea. Usually the trigger person isn't naturally organized, so the organizers come along and work with the idea until it is functional. A ministry needs managers as well. These people run with the organized big idea and mobilize the final type of person: the worker. The workers carry out the new ministry on a day-to-day basis.

When a team of people hears God together, you will find the necessary individuals with the gifts and abilities to mobilize a ministry that in turn meets needs and reaches people for Christ. The body of Christ is an organism. We're all different and respond to God differently, and this is essential in the body of Christ—no one person can fulfill all its functions. The church must simply create a place where people resonating with a new idea can come alongside each other and carry out God's purpose and will in their lives and in the life of the church.

If a team of people is gathered and it appears all the pieces are in place to move forward with this new ministry idea, we bless them to move on. However, as in the case of unmet parameters, if no one appears to be responding to the big idea yet, we ask the trigger person to wait for at least six months or more and try again.

Finally, these simple processes described above also benefits the leadership team. This practical approach to testing stirred individuals keeps pressure on and off the leadership team in all the right places. For instance, there's no pressure upon them to understand everything the Lord is doing in the midst of His church. They have freedom not to know the future direction of the church. Secondly, there's no pressure to recruit for a ministry—no reason for those in leadership to coerce the congregation into action. At MAC we stress that if a ministry or need resonates deeply within the hearts of those in the church, then those individuals have the responsibility to the Spirit to take action. In response, the leadership team must not quench the work of the Spirit. This is the right kind of pressure to keep on a leadership team.

Remember, a need never constitutes call. In 2005, the district leadership called our attention to another Christian and Missionary Alliance church on the verge of shutting down. At this point, our internship program had produced a number of pastors and church planters. District leadership hoped a team from MAC would start something new in a building that housed a dying church. It appeared to make logical sense.

Instead of forcing a great idea that clearly lined up with God's word, I wanted God to lead us. The leadership team and I waited, prayed, and practiced relaxed concern.

Two years later, with no mention of my conversation with the district to those in the church, an assembly of people was organically gathering. A new crop of interns approached me with the desire to apply what they were learning in their classes to real-life situations—they wanted to plant a church. Simultaneously, families from the community of the dying church began commuting to MAC for services and they later began a home group. Perhaps God had gathered the right people at the right time to build up a nearby church. To test this new direction, I talked privately with the interns and the new home group about the prospects. They wanted to move forward with the plant, and the time appeared to be right. I told our district superintendent we would pursue their original request. At the time of this writing, we are still practicing relaxed concern.

As we follow Him, we ride on the momentum of His plan and provision, not on "someone ought to" motivation. Just because we have started out on the right foot doesn't mean the road ahead will be smooth. The future is murky and I'm not confident about all the details. Struggles and failures will crop up in this new adventure. Yet in the end, we expect Him to do great and unique things among us because He is the one who started it. And of course, He wants it more than we do.

Questions for Reflection

1. Identify the struggles you have living between a promise and the fulfillment of that promise.

2. There are more needs than we can meet. How does relaxed concern protect us from good causes?

3. What current ministries are striving in human effort?

4. How does your church decide which ministries they will pursue?

CHAPTER 7

VIEWING A NEW DESTINATION THROUGH PRAYER

During a unique period of time at MAC, we experienced rapid growth, limited staff, and a small population of middle and high school students. The end result was a church with no youth group. For being an established church, this was an odd characteristc—one that surprised many who visited us. A few eventually voiced concern over the missing ministry, and in response I called a prayer meeting for the church to seek the Lord on the matter.

In minutes, the prayer meeting turned into a town hall meeting. Everyone interested voiced their opinions until the group divided down the middle. Those who wanted the youth group cited these kids needed biblical teaching specific to adolescent needs, such as relationships with the opposite sex and purity. Those who thought a youth ministry was unnecessary explained the New Testament church did not seem to value separating the church by age—besides, the present youth seemed to be acclimating well as they grew into maturity alongside the adults.

Both were great points. Both sides made good biblical sense.

Instead of taking a vote and letting the majority decide, I wanted the Lord to guide this decision. I stopped the debate and ended the meeting by asking everyone to lay their intentions down. I prayed God would lead us to what He wanted for our community and for our youth. The next week, we continued our prayer meeting. The second time around, we entered His presence differently. In one hand we loosely held our preconceived notions and requests; in the other we offered Him space to come and speak as to how we should proceed.

God will be faithful to draw our attention to the work He has for us while we pray, but most often churches pray as though the entire burden of His work rests squarely upon our shoulders. Our prayers share the tendencies of Nimrod as he set out to build Babel; they have an "it is up to us" attitude and it ushers Jesus right out the front door of His church.

When it comes to communicating with God, we in the church have forced prayer into roles outside of what God intended.

In some churches there is a sense that we must repeatedly ask and plead with God so that He will show up and fulfill our requests. This is a works-based perspective on prayer. A church moves into dangerous territory when she acts as if God won't move unless she puts in x amount of hours on her knees. In this situation, prayer functions as currency. If we pay God enough, He'll do what we ask.

Somewhat related are those in the word-of-faith camp I briefly mentioned in an earlier chapter. They believe if you pray and confess correctly, God is obligated to do whatever you request—it is as if His hands are tied by our skillful entreaties. As the puppeteer, we control the strings, and dangling at the end of them we find God in the role of the puppet.

In equally dangerous territory is the self-reliant church. This church might dream about what they want to look like in five years and then re-verse-engineer a plan to bring them to that end. They might also borrow ideas and ministries from other successful churches to target a specific group in hopes of boosting numbers. Instead of ideas and new direction being birthed during prayer, the church asks God to bless the ideas they've already set in place. In this example, prayer functions as a mindless routine, an afterthought, or even worse, a garnish—only meant for spiritually aesthetic purposes.

I am not suggesting it is inappropriate to come to God with requests. God's purpose for prayer leaves ample space for our requests when they are free from functioning like currency, string-directing a marionette, or merely garnishing our own plans. However, more is available for the church when we pray. Opening the door to Jesus and believing "God wants it more than we do" will naturally change how we view prayer in our churches. Prayer will begin to change us and our perspective. Prayer will begin to transform our thinking. In this posture of dependence, there is freedom to be surprised by His unique plans for the church.

Before the Foundations of the World

What a relief God is not limited to our prayers. The life and well-being of the church is not dependent upon the wisdom of men, but on the power of God. Paul reminds us in 1 Corinthians 2:9: "'No eye has seen, no ear has heard, no mind has conceived what God has prepared for those who love him,' *but God has revealed it to us by his Spirit. The Spirit searches all things, even the deep things of God.*"[29] In His innermost parts, God has unbelievably great plans for the church. How could man ever expect to anticipate these deep things of God? Thankfully, the Spirit is our link. He reveals the deepest desires of God to the minds and hearts of believers.

In this context of 1 Corinthians 2:9, Paul is speaking of the glorious Messiah and the life-giving mystery He unfolded—man's reconciliation to God through the forgiveness of sins. No one could have expected something so wonderful. God destined the message of salvation through His Son before time began. Then He hid the plan, waiting for the right time to reveal it. Catching everyone unawares, the Spirit unveiled parts of the mystery to some: Mary, Elizabeth, and their husbands. God prepared a few to receive the promise and one would literally give birth to this special promise.

The same is true for our churches today. Of course, the plan of salvation has been fully revealed to us and it is no longer a mystery. But

God still has purposes for His local churches—purposes He has destined before the foundations of the world. Furthermore, He is preparing many in these churches to receive these promises from His Holy Spirit. Currently unknown to us, these promises will transform our thinking and uniquely build the church God so desperately loves.

How do we learn of these promises, believe them, receive them corporately as a church, and watch them come into fruition? As I mentioned before, we have to understand that our times of prayer in the church are not only about requests, but also a time for God to meet with us, reposition us, and let us in on the plans He has for the church.

Conceived of the Holy Spirit

First, I must make myself clear: God doesn't always reveal His plans through prayer. Sometimes He drags us into His will as He did with me and the unsigned contract and cookie lady. However, as I reflect on the history of MAC, most of what has transpired here—the ministry training program, the coupling of business and ministry, the multisite church model—first emerged during prayers. These ideas were not birthed in board meetings or brainstorming sessions with the staff or even out of my own hopes and dreams for the church. God went beyond what anyone could have asked or imagined. We currently run a course conceived by the Holy Spirit, not by man. Upon reflection, I notice the life of MAC has resembled the life of Mary in a lot of key ways.

The account of Luke tells us the angel Gabriel unexpectedly visited Mary and told her she would give birth to the Son of God. Notice how God is the active character in the story. Mary is on the receiving end and responds in kind: "I am the Lord's servant."[30] The beginning of a marvelous plan started without the direct action of a human. She was available, not asking for anything, and then all of a sudden God visits, God creates, and God initiates.

Muncie Alliance believes God still initiates today. We are not so much charismatic in our expression, but we do believe in the gifts of the

Spirit. Furthermore we are open to God utilizing them when He wants to reveal His deep-seated plans for us. As I have told you, God has spoken interesting promises to us and we have seen them come to pass. This confirms there is validity to the gifts of the Spirit despite many in the church taking a hands-off approach to them or denying their existence altogether.

One way to hear God is through the gifts—through words of knowledge, prophecy, dreams, or visions. But even as radical as this may sound to some, it doesn't have to be the kooky, weird process many have made it out to be, such as hyping up a service with meaningless repetitions and chanting in order to work themselves into a "spiritual" state. It's abusive when those in the church hide behind a so-called prophecy and use it to confront or to manipulate circumstances and people. And I don't think a demon is to blame every time something bad or even marginally unfortunate happens. I've never experienced God's presence through lightning bolts or audible voices, and I don't think we should expect that. In the most general of terms, when I say we are open to the gifts manifesting, I mean we go before God and listen. We still ourselves and pay attention to Him. We are sensitive to strong impressions or pictures in our mind's eye that unfold a new perspective. Simple pictures, like spider webs, give analogies that help us to line up with God's purposes and desires.

Being open to the gifts places us in a posture of dependency; we are the ones meant to receive, not conceive. Instead of relying upon a list of requests when we pray, we are asking God to set the tone, the pace, and the subject matter of our prayers. Furthermore, the more we practice listening, the more we learn to recognize God's voice.

Belief

Once Mary heard the promise, she then took a step of faith and believed the wild things Gabriel told her. Let's not downplay this step of faith. She understood enough biology to rationally reject Gabriel's message. The fact that she was a virgin didn't add up with Gabriel's claim that she was now pregnant. Yet she responded: "May it be to me as you have said."[31]

When God spoke to me through the spider web analogy, I remember thinking: *You want to put a church here for the world to see? There are only forty-five people and over half want to fire me.* From what I could tell, God's promise seemed to be a long shot.

In the midst of lots of questions and a bleary future, we must believe. If we take God at His word, our hearts and minds are repositioned. The next time we face a decision in the church, we will proceed with the option that best lines up with God's promise. After the spider web encounter, I believed God would set up a delicate network as we did the things He had written across the hearts of His people. As opportunities for regional roasting arise for Alliance World Coffees, we feel we have His permission and the freedom to pursue them. When God opens doors in other cities and countries for another site church, we move with Him as He builds His church. Now others have noticed God's work in our midst. Each year pastors from around the globe attend the Beeson Institute at Asbury Seminary in Wilmore, Kentucky. They travel throughout the US, visiting different types of churches. One of the stops is MAC, fulfilling the promise God spoke: *I'm going to put a church here for the world to see.* Ultimately, faith in God's promises will guide us to the manifestation of that promise.

Secondly, when we believe, we live in expectation. God wants to see the promise come to pass more than we do (otherwise, why would He waste His time telling us about it?). Therefore, we can expect Him to bring about the right people and circumstances to bring us to that end. When I'm on board with what God wants and I'm expecting Him to move, I am now in a position to notice opportunities and people that would have normally slid by undetected—especially if I'd had only my own desires in mind. Believing the promises aligns us with God desires. We have no idea how it will play out in the end, but we're set up on a course to watch the promises unfold. This is a blessed place to be. As Mary believed, Elizabeth said, "Blessed is she who believed that there would be a fulfillment of what had been spoken to her by the Lord."[32]

Confirmation

Take another cue from Mary: Live in a place where the promise is validated and encouraged. In conjunction with her own news, the angel revealed the news of her Aunt Elizabeth. At once Mary left for Judah where Elizabeth lived. When Mary arrived and greeted her aunt, Elizabeth's baby leapt in her womb and she began prophesying. "Blessed are you among women, and blessed is the fruit of your womb! And how has it happened to me that the mother of my Lord would come to me?"[33] Elizabeth's words legitimized and validated what God began in Mary. Over the next three months, they could talk freely about their hopes and concerns, their fears and joys that precious few could wholly understand.

Hanging around other people of promise fosters the promise in our own hearts and minds. This type of community will encourage one another, nurture the promise in its new and delicate state, and carry each other through until the time it unfolds.

A weekly prayer meeting at MAC began to function as a fostering community. We gathered to worship God and intercede, and then we quieted ourselves to give God permission to speak to us. He would speak simple words of hope or healing to some, or birth new ideas and direction for the church. When the latter began to repeatedly happen, we dubbed the meeting room the Birthing Room.

Not only was the Birthing Room a place to hear God, but for promises to be confirmed. When God spoke through pictures or impressions, people felt safe to speak of what they were seeing and how it might relate to a promise. Often, there were others who saw the same things and came to the same conclusions on their own. As we talked and shared, promises were validated and new perspectives were adopted. On the flip side, there were times when people spoke up, but no one else received the same impressions. The community, in this way, also tested the gifts. If someone "missed" God, no blame was laid, there was freedom to fail as well as freedom to learn how to hear and recognize God's voice.

Another reason to place yourself in a community that fosters promise, like the Birthing Room, is so the work of the Spirit can be caught and owned by others. Just because He speaks directly to a few does not mean that only those few will be involved in God's plans. God spoke to me about the stacked deck and spider web, but those who have joined MAC years later have accepted God's message to me as their own inheritance. They believe God could be bringing them to MAC to minister in ways already on the heart of God but beyond what any of us are thinking or dreaming. Furthermore, all six site churches that have launched out from MAC have not only inherited the promises but also claim the promises of the stacked deck and the spider web for themselves. Now they too expect God to fulfill His words in their own midst.

Birth

The birth is the most exciting part. This is the time we get to see God's plans realized in our midst. This is the point, the goal, the reason why we listen while we pray. We listen so we can experience the yield of the Holy Spirit. We listen to see something unique develop in our midst, beyond what we were thinking and planning: a Holy Spirit original.

When Mary gave birth to Jesus, in the simplest of terms, she brought forth life. Jesus wants to bring life into His church—unique, vibrant life that has organic momentum and whisks people into purpose and focus. The type of momentum exhibited in the early New Testament church. As God brings forth life, we won't be able to believe our eyes and ears. Our hearts will overflow as we witness that which God has prepared. And don't even try to put perimeters on His plans because they just might change the whole world.

I never set out to have a multi-site church, or to stumble upon pairing business with ministry. The current profile of MAC never entered into my heart or mind, therefore I couldn't pray about it—but prayer was part of the process. We didn't view prayer as a garnish, not an exercise to bring about what we wanted, but a time to be enlarged, to see God's perspective and accept what He wants to do. We allowed prayer to change us and set us on a new course.

Questions for Reflection

1. Share about something birthed in prayer. Discuss an event garnished in prayer. What was the outcome of each?

2. How, like Elizabeth, are you supporting people living in unfulfilled promise?

CHAPTER 8

CALLING OUT GOD'S LEADERS

Remember the Magic Eye craze of the '90s? Stores cropped up in malls across the country filled with books, postcards, posters, and even neckties devoted to these colorful stereograms—two-dimensional color patterns arranged to give the illusion of depth. Passersby would see the same scene in the showroom: groups staring at posters speckled with color. Everyone stood cross-eyed and silent until one would exclaim, "Oh! I see it! It's a bird!" "Where? Where?" the others crowded in. The finder would motion and describe to the seekers until they saw the bird in flight as well.

The trick was to focus your eyes differently. Normally when we look at a photograph or a painting or a postcard, we glance and our brain instantly processes what is before us. We see our children, a ship at sea, or the New York skyline without thinking much about it. To make sense of the organized smears of a Magic Eye poster, you had to refocus your eyes. Once you did, a three-dimensional image jumped out from a paper-thin poster. Upon learning the trick, the eye began to see an image that had always been present. With practice, you could process a Magic Eye poster as quickly as grandma's photos from last Christmas because your eyes had been retrained to see.

Pastor as Coach and Equipper

Through the difficult circumstances of MAC's past, God retrained my eyes. As God stacked the deck I began to see the church with fresh eyes. Instead of driving my plan from my seat atop the organizational chart or delegating my list of tasks to others, I began to expect God to show up and directly shape His church through circumstances and people. I began to keep watch for those whom God awakened to serve in His vineyard. Believing God would build His church, Christ's words in John 5:17 came alive. "My Father is always at work to this very day, and I, too, am working."[34] Just like the Magic Eye posters, the image of a vibrant church jumped out from the overworked patterns.

I began to grasp my own limitations. If Jesus had this to say about himself—"I tell you the truth, the Son can do *nothing by himself*; He can do only what he sees His Father doing, because whatever the Father does the Son also does"—then how much more would my aims apart from the Father come to nothing?[35] The story of how the internship started through acquisition of the roaster solidified my desire to stop driving my ambitious plans in hopes of conjuring up excitement and momentum in the church. I would wait. When I saw God move, I would run after His progress—and this would be enough to book my schedule.

This perspective took some pressure off me. I didn't have to know the destination of the church. I didn't have to have a five-year plan. Christ is committed to building His church and He will move us to that end. I simply needed to ensure that we, as a church, were prepared to follow Him. Not called to be a CEO or a hireling, I stepped into my new role as a coach and equipper. I began to expect God to whisper to the hearts of His children, to call them to action, and to lift them up to serve.

The church adopted the characteristics of a grassroots movement. Upon the Spirit's leading, the constituents of the community, so to speak, held the means to shape the future of the church. This new potential of the congregation differed from MAC's previous congregation with a traditional church mentality. Instead of their actions growing out of a sense of guardianship over the church, the new community was motivated to act by Christ stirring them to do the things He had written across their hearts. The new directions and changes in the church happened naturally and spontaneously as people spoke up and did the things they were purposed to do.

I became intentional about identifying sons and daughters in the faith to train and to help grow into the fullness of stature which belongs to Christ. I searched within the church for ministry leaders and staff instead of hiring someone on the outside who looked good on paper. Homegrown leadership isn't always a clean and simple way of doing things. Messy ministry may be uncomfortable, but I'd rather see believers learn how to lead with some mess than bypass them in the name of excellence. For Christians who want to see God use them, it is difficult to receive the message they are not trained enough or experienced enough to minister.

In some ways, my friend Darren lived under the burden of not being quite good enough in the eyes of others. Hired as a youth pastor in a church who valued a seminary education and denominational licensing, his business and marketing degree worked against him in the church. Darren quickly burnt out as superiors frequently rechecked his work and vetoed his ministry ideas. He and his wife Nancy decided to take a break from ministry and focus on the family bookstore business. Years before, while Darren was an undergraduate, Judy and I had met him at a Valentine's Day banquet we catered at his college. When he opened his first store, he and Nancy tracked us down to shop from our line of espresso machines for their café. Servicing their machine in the following years provided the time and excuse to keep in touch. Our entrepreneurial spirits and belief in a lay movement provided a common ground for friendship. They showed up at our doors one Sunday morning, eight years after the Valentine's Day banquet, exhausted and beaten-up by ministry. Darren and his family needed time to regroup, but I think we both knew he would relaunch into ministry one day.

Two other men in the midst of MAC caught my eye as potential pastors. Matt was a passionate young man and a great communicator, but another youth pastor heading for burnout. He shuffled through our doors between jobs and during a spiritual and personal low point in his life. Since he jetted around the country nearly every weekend for job interviews, he and I met during the week in a local coffee shop to talk about life and our perspectives on ministry. He carried such a deeply philosophical view of the church as a whole, that I questioned whether being a youth pastor was the best fit for him. I spoke to him about becoming a pastor, but my suggestions were quickly dismissed in view of the lineup of potential jobs. All his leads eventually fell through and one day he began to reconsider my proddings.

A young musician by the name of Josh Garrels came to faith and was discipled at MAC. He eventually dropped out of college to join the MAC internship. Because his spiritual growth happened before my eyes, in some respects I viewed him as a son. I even fell into the father/son routine by getting on his case about his church responsibilities like replacing light bulbs and locking doors. Then I attended one of his CD release concerts. I saw him differently as he commanded the attention of a large crowd. After the concert, I felt as though I needed to get in line for his autograph. During his second year as an intern, he taught a class on the book of Revelation for an assignment. Sensing he might be a gifted teacher, I decided to test it out. On Sunday nights when I couldn't lead our coffeehouse church plant in Indy, I asked Josh to fill in. He did so well, soon enough I was looking for excuses to miss the Sunday night gathering.

By this time in the history of MAC, the internship had survived four years and the church had moved out of the old, cramped sanctuary into a spacious auditorium. Students poured in from area colleges in three Indiana cities—Upland, Anderson, and Marion—and once again we ran out of space. The prospect of another building project did not interest me for many reasons. I didn't want to become a loosely connected, behemoth of a church. Additionally, we recently planted a church in Huntington, Indiana, and my intern coordinator left his post to pastor the plant. The demands of the internship fell into my lap where I already held the responsibilities of senior pastor and church planter in Indy. This was no time for another building project.

This was an opportunity to see where God was leading His church next.

I sized up the situation God had led us into: Each Sunday the church building filled to capacity. Many of the congregants commuted from a forty-five-minute radius. I am a coach and and a equipper, not a one-man-show. Three men in the MAC community are called to be pastors.

Instead of the congregation migrating to Muncie every Sunday for church, what if we moved the church out to the congregation? I wondered. MAC could meet in multiple communities around central Indiana. In place of relocating each week to be a part of a body of believers, students from the surrounding areas could stay put on Sunday mornings and be the church in their own backyard. While the presence of the students added strength and vitality to our church body, I wondered if they could impact their communities more effectively by being the church where they lived and worked.

The students, however, commuted to Muncie because they were attracted to MAC's values. The new communities needed to share our same values or it wouldn't be long before the worshipers returned to Muncie. Pastors and leaders who attended MAC and bought into the MAC value system would be the key to a successful transition to this multi-site model. The pieces of this puzzle were falling into place. Three pastors, Darren, Matt, and Josh, were available to serve.

Granted, they weren't ready to go it alone. They'd need some coaching, but I believed in them. They just needed to be appointed. Josh was the clear choice for Indy, Matt for Anderson, and Darren in Upland/Gas City. In one summer, we launched three new sites, giving away three leaders and hundreds of worshipers. Thanks to God's lead, MAC now is in a habit of sending out pastors and church planting teams. To date, MAC meets in six different sites across Indiana.

Identity Transformation

In Darren's past experience, he had served under those who valued credentials over call. The leadership of the church believed it was up to them to build the church. In this instance, their perspective played out in how they treated their staff. Mimicking the business world, they trusted in qualifications and experience. Since Darren lacked both, they kept him on a tight leash in order to protect their church. In other professional churches, a person can't even serve in a ministry without the proper degree and ministry background.

The professional way of appointing staff—sifting through résumés for the well-educated and experienced—would have eliminated most of the leaders in the early church. For instance, in Acts 4 we find Peter and John preaching and healing the sick in the temple and the authorities quickly arresting them. Bringing them before the high priest, they asked the two men by what power they had done these things. The Holy Spirit fell upon Peter and he began to reason with the men. "When they saw the courage of Peter and John and realized that they were unschooled, ordinary men, they were astonished and they took note that these men had been with Jesus."[36]

This is not the only instance in which the unschooled and ordinary were called to do the work of the Kingdom. God called others, not because of what they accomplished, but because of what God had written across their hearts. My favorite story in all of scripture, Philip the table-waiter-turned-evangelist, backs up this perspective as well.

In Acts 8, the apostles, by this time renowned and well-respected, remained in Jerusalem while the Spirit moved beyond the borders of the holy city. God didn't send the professionals to speak the truth of the Gospel; He sent a lay movement. This man Philip, who served meals to widows by day, spoke up about Jesus after the persecution transplanted him. His audience, the Samaritans, listened because the works of God followed him—he cast out demons and healed the lame. A city trapped under bondage inhaled the breath of freedom for the first time and exhaled with much rejoicing. Philip was only one of many scattered proclaiming the good news. God was using a lay movement of everyday people to redeem the world to Himself.

Jesus gives the following promise to *everyone* who calls Him Lord: "But you will receive power when the Holy Spirit comes on you; and you will be My witnesses in Jerusalem, in all of Judea, and Samaria, and to the ends of the earth."[37] God is not concerned with accomplishments and failures, our answers or lack thereof. If He goes with us, incredible things will happen.

I think Philip saw himself differently after he stepped up to the challenge and God used a simple water boy to bring great joy in Samaria. As he moved away from home base, he was unable to leave the job to someone else. He had to fulfill the role as evangelist and healer. Likewise, sometimes God orchestrates events in our lives, pushing us into circumstances where we are in over our heads. Because our typical response is hampered, we see God filling in our deficiencies in ways we've never experienced before. In those times, God will not only show us who He is but also who He purposed us to be. We will begin to view ourselves differently. The next time we step out in faith, we expect to be used by God. The limits that once held us captive are broken as God begins to do incredibly more than we could ever ask or think, through ordinary people like you and me.

If we trust in pieces of paper filled out in beautiful calligraphy and stamped with gold seals or an impressive track record, we will miss out on God building His church in impressive ways through simple and ordinary people. We need to be about recognizing the leaders God has already assembled among us within the local church.

Identifying Leaders

In Ephesians 4:7-16 Paul says Christ measured out additional grace to believers. He gifted us all with tools to fulfill the work of the Kingdom. Out of all of us, some will receive a portion of grace large enough to be apostles, prophets, evangelists, pastors, or teachers. Christ hands these leadership roles out so that these leaders can, in turn, equip the rest of the church for works of service. Some of us may not be used to seeing this biblical model lived out in practical ways. Congregations are accustomed to sitting back and allowing those with a so-called special call to serve, typically understood to be the pastor, some teachers, and/or a few missionaries. Paul contradicts this point in this section of scripture. The work set before the leaders—the apostles, prophets, evangelists, pastors, and teachers—is not to do all the work of the church, but to equip the saints to do so. Then, in turn, the saints will do the works of service. Each part of the body of Christ has work to do and each part must do his or her job in order for the church to be healthy—just like our human bodies. Once everyone in the body is serving, the body works together in harmony and purpose, supporting each other and building each other up in love as we all do the work God set before us.

In light of this section of Ephesians, the leadership is responsible to identify those who are stirred, called, and lifted up by the Spirit to equip the saints and build up His church. As a pastor, I am called to be a coach and an equipper—equipping those in my congregation for service. I am to train those in my charge and to release them for works of service. The work set before me is to discover God's leaders and encourage them to live out their purpose and calling.

Paul, as an apostle, practiced what he preached and monitored his churches, looking for God's leaders. Circling around Asia Minor during his second missionary journey, he met a prospective leader, a man named Timothy. He was well spoken of by those in the church and Paul decided to invite him along for the ride.

There are other ways to identify God's leaders. Darren's honest desire to serve the Lord and his passion to do the things God had written across his heart were obvious as we chatted over coffee. As a coach and equipper, I knew I had a responsibility to encourage his desire and passion and to challenge him to serve. I'd walk alongside him and watch for any opportunities God brought about in His church.

In the past, finding potential leaders was as simple as reading a few of the ministry forms I mentioned in an earlier chapter.

I found some leaders in a somewhat unlikely place: those giving constructive criticism. As a pastor, one can be easily jaded by the volume of unsolicited comments and advice. This use to put me on the defensive as I took it personally. Once my perspectives on who builds the church began to shift and I realized the church wasn't mine to build or guard, I was less apt to be offended by people's comments. To those who were overly critical, I dismissed their comments until they learned more humility. But to those whose suggestions were heartfelt and selfless, I began to listen more closely. They stretched my thinking and challenged me to do things differently. Once I gave them credence, I realized these people would make great leaders.

Sometimes I've even received God's perspective through prophetic means to help me identify leaders. This isn't a new concept. Paul often mentioned the prophecies spoken over Timothy as he encouraged him in his work at Ephesus. "This command I entrust to you, Timothy, my son, in accordance with the prophecies previously made concerning you…"[38] Later in the same letter Paul reminded him: "Do not neglect the spirtiual gift within you, which was bestowed on you through prophetic utterance with the laying on of hands…"[39]

One Sunday I briefly spoke about lay ministry and how college and seminary degrees aren't necessary to be able to minister in the body of Christ. I suggested that sometimes it would be better to quit school than to incur thousands of dollars of debt and be enslaved by this financial responsibility as you begin to minister. I spent only a few minutes on this topic but it was enough to stir one of the hearts in the congregation. After the service, Dave walked up to the front for prayer. We had never met before and the only introduction I received that morning was: "I've been thinking about quitting school. I met Josh Garrels at his last concert and he told me about the MAC internship. I might join so that I can be a pastor someday. Would you pray for me?"

I placed my hand upon his head and said a few words. Moments later, the Holy Spirit came. Dave later told me his heart began to beat faster and his whole body felt shaky, like in instances when someone is extremely nervous. As the Holy Spirit was ministering, I felt prompted to say, "Just let it go." Without me knowing how, this spoke directly to Dave's heart as he was struggling to give up his electrical engineering degree and a guaranteed paycheck.

This moment was an important one for the both of us. For Dave, this was a turning point in his life. He let go of the life he had planned. He quit his coursework at Purdue University and joined the MAC internship. God used that time of prayer to identify another one of His leaders to me. I now knew of another leader to take into my charge, speaking into his life and encouraging him to follow the path God had marked out for him.

God will build His church. He will unearth people to serve His purposes. If we truly believe this perspective, we will look for and identify those God has called to build His church.

Test, Train, and Equip the Saints

One year into our new internship program, our internship coordinator Chad left MAC to plant a church in Huntington, Indiana. He had been running the entire program and his absence left a major void. Previously, I had simply showed up to teach my classes. After his departure, the prospect of teaching all the classes plus dealing with all the organizational details left me greatly overwhelmed—anyone who has ever spent a few minutes with me can attest I am embarassingly disorganized. I remember taking the victim's stance: "God, why would you do this to me?" His miraculous provisions to begin the program only fueled my frustrations as to why He would drop out at this moment when the internship was so young and vulnerable.

Again God was up to something good, we just didn't recognize it at the time. He was dragging us into His will kicking and screaming. I could have quickly hired another coordinator, but that would have gone against all God had taught us up to that point. With no better alternatives, I sat down with the second-year interns and explained I needed help. I ask them to divide up some of the classes and to teach the first-year students.

After the meeting, I remember being nervous this idea would implode, but resigned to the fact that I did the best I could on a limited timetable. But I was surprised to find that some of the students were passionate about teaching—even some of the more introverted students. Furthermore, the teaching by the second-years deeply ministered to the first-year interns. I had failed to view this development of the internship from God's perspective. As it turned out, the idea worked out better than we all expected.

Experiencing the success of our Plan B, I realized it was actually biblical and we should have expected it to work all along. Paul had only recently met Timothy when he invited him along on his second missionary journey. To his credit, Timothy was a believer and well spoken of by those who knew him, but he lacked formal training and experiences that would have made him an obvious choice to be Paul's protégé. Paul identified Timothy as a leader because God had chosen him as one, and credentials aside, Paul invited him along on a mission trip for exposure. This would turn out to be the best training of all. Timothy learned by watching and doing.

As Chad followed his call elsewhere, God helped us stumble upon the Hebraic model of teaching at MAC. This model is based heavily upon teaching as you go, or teaching as a group collectively experiences something. Throughout the Gospels, Jesus often taught the disciples through this model of show and tell. Without much thought as to *how* to teach the interns, the original structure of the program mimicked the Greek model: an expert lecturing a group of beginners. Through a supposed setback, the program gained balance. Now, not only would the internship teach the tenants of the faith and delve into the theoretical (even Jesus chose to do this from time to time), but it would also train the students through real-life experiences. The internship would simultaneously teach and test the students in preparation for ministry.

One of the marks of a church following God's plans is the provision of opportunities to test and train potential leaders. As I mentioned before, the second-year interns did a great job teaching their assigned classes, so I asked some to teach MAC's midweek studies. We've seen professionals in the workplace volunteer to lead a home group or take on the challenge to teach a midweek study. Now one is sensing a call to lead a new MAC site church. Whatever the case, we attempt to set people up for success by starting them out with something small, and then slowly moving them to take on larger responsibilities. However, there isn't a set course or list of tasks one must complete in order to gain more responsibility. The mechanism is flexible enough to bend to each individual and mold to his or her special circumstances and needs.

I have to touch on the point that creating this mechanism to find and test leaders happened *after* leaders were surfacing. Form followed function. We didn't sit down and plan out how we could test, train, and equip leaders; the mechanism emerged naturally after leaders appeared and we faithfully stewarded their talents. A word of caution: Don't seek to copy this model in hopes of drumming up leaders. Instead, watch for those whom God awakened to serve in His vineyard and seek out how to steward their gifts—whether it be through a new ministry or one that is already in place—by testing them, training them, and equipping them.

Launch and Apply

God will assemble new leaders within His church. Once He does, will those in leadership positions offer places for them to serve? Identifying and equipping other leaders in the church takes a bit of sacrifice on the part of the pastor or anyone else who is responsible for a ministry and recognizes leaders under his or her care. We have to learn to share. Sometimes we will need to loosen our grip on part of the ministry so that others can lend a hand and live out their calling alongside us. Routinely checking the desires of our hearts is important. Deep inside do we love titles, authority, attention, and being needed? Have we become territorial within the church? Letting the church go is difficult for insecure pastors who are threatened by people with giftedness.

Speaking from my own experience, I have had to set aside my fears and insecurities. In a previous church, I experienced a bitter congregational coup and from that wound I became suspicious of congregations. I needed to let go of my misgivings and speak into the lives of those in the congregation without worrying they would gain strength and boot me out of a job. Most recently, I've had to deal with different insecurities. Many of the site pastors are younger, hipper, and smarter than me. They've had more education, they are well-spoken, and better organized. Compared to me they appear better equipped to lead a church. But God has a place for us all. He doesn't run the church like a cruelly pragmatic HR department, only concerned with the bottom line where the more gifted people replace the less gifted. I am sure God has securely placed me as the pastor of MAC. Consequently, I share the role of teacher for time to time so others can have the opportunity to teach. Instead of pastoring a church in the thousands back when MAC had outgrown our new auditorium, I entrusted parts of the congregation to three young men so that they could live out their calls as pastors. The church must learn to share and entrust parts of herself to the laity if we desire to be poised and ready to follow God wherever He leads us.

When God led Darren to MAC, I identified him as God's leader. In passing I'd mention how I thought he would minister again some day in the future. Later, I asked him to fill in at midweek studies when I was out of town—he was great! The time had come to launch him into ministry. The next Sunday I announced Darren would be the pastor of the Exit 59 church—I just hadn't spoken to him about it yet. He was equally dumbfounded as his wife Nancy, slightly frustrated, elbowed him whispering, "Why didn't you tell me?"

It was time for him to live out his call, regardless of his fears, his insecurities, and the inadequacies he felt. In a complete about-face from his experiences in the past, someone was asking Darren to serve because of call, not because of credentials.

Nurture

I basically pushed Darren, Matt, and Josh into the roles of the three new site pastors. They felt too young and were unsure if they could handle such a huge responsibility. Two of the guys freaked out about teaching through the Bible chapter by chapter, verse by verse—a value we hold at MAC. They preferred to speak topically. MAC had worked through the entire New Testament and was ready to tackle the book of Revelation. This meant we'd take an entire Sunday service to discuss the church of Smyrna.

"How am I going to do a whole message on four verses?" one pointedly asked.

"Don't worry," I consoled. "We'll do this together."

We planned to launch the new sites in the fall, so during the summer we all met to study the portion of scripture to be taught the following Sunday. Each person had at least one opportunity to preach what we had studied during a Sunday morning service. Pretty soon, the guys really enjoyed our weekly studies. They would study on their own before we met on Wednesday mornings and bring in information about historical context and compare and contrast what other commentators had to say about the text. *I could get used to this.* Never had I been so excited to prepare my teaching, and never had I had access to so much information!

Again, we stumbled upon another plan God had to build up MAC. Our Wednesday morning meeting lasted well past that first summer. After the launches, we continued to meet together. It became an obvious place to discuss practical issues such as: "What do you do when there are character issues within the leadership team?" "How do I purchase a building?" "What do I do when people within the congregation want to sue each other?"

Not only has our meeting displayed longevity, but it has also grown in numbers. We invite other teachers who attend MAC but aren't currently called to be a site pastor (yet) and other pastors in the area. Nearly every week someone new is visiting. Studying scripture with multiple perspectives at the table has been healthy for us as individual pastors as well. We've let go of our pet doctrines and natural tendencies as different perspectives and disagreements cause us to delve deeper into the text and to understand what it is truly saying. We call our meeting the Teaching Pool—a place where we pool our ideas, thoughts, questions, and facts. Additionally, it's a pool of teachers, or a place to find a substitute when a pastor is out of town.

The genius of the Teaching Pool—the Spirit's genious we happened to stumble upon—is the community. Pastoring, normally a solo affair, is done in the midst of community. We stay connected as a church body. When needs arise in one place, now six other sites are available to lend a helping hand. When one site is called to send a team to Africa, six other sites hear about it and can share their funds and their congregations. The Teaching Pool also connects the pastors. We laugh together, mourn together, rejoice together, keep each other accountable, and confess to one another. And when one of us has had enough and we want to wash our hands of this call and walk away, we remind each other to fight the good fight. Paul did the same to Timothy when he was struggling to lead the church in Ephesus. He reminds him not to neglect the gift Christ had apportioned to him.[40]

Identifying, training, and launching leaders will be in vain if the church fails to nurture them once they have stepped out in faith. Be watching for ways the Spirit might be creatively leading you to nurture your leaders.

God is faithful to send budding leaders to His churches. In light of this, a healthy church is a safe haven for inexperienced leaders to grow and to flourish. In the Kingdom of God, there is no room for posturing for position or neglecting those with giftedness until they leave in frustration.

Established leaders in a healthy church will speak into the lives of budding leaders just as Paul spoke into the life of Timothy. The "Pauls," so to speak, will believe in the "Timothys" as they are emerging—despite their initial ineffectiveness and even if everything is messy. Trading in the image of a polished and slick church is worth the end result of raising new leaders. Give the Timothys opportunities in small and increasing ways to help them learn and grow into stronger leaders. Walk alongside them by mentoring and nurturing them until they are an established leader—until they take on the role of a Paul and eventually call out a new Timothy.

Questions for Reflection

1. How can you recognize who God is raising up?

2. How can we nurture leaders *in the context* of the church?

3. Are there mechanisms in place to test and launch emerging leaders?

4. Am I willing to share ministry with emerging leaders?

CHAPTER 9

GOD'S ECONOMY OF FAILURE

No church wants to wholeheartedly commit to an original idea, applying her time and emotional and physical energy to it, only to see it come to nothing. You're viewed as the group who couldn't seal the deal. You fell short of expectations. Competence is questioned. Ability appears to be lacking. You're disappointed, you feel defeated, and you've caused a setback. Without an end product and nothing tangible to point to at the end of months and months of hard work, we're relunctant to try again. We're paralyzed by fear.

The pain of failure provokes us to avoid it in the future. We minimize risks. Next time we'll send out more feelers in our attempt to better gauge what the public is looking for. Next time we'll be sure to have a stronger, smarter team working behind us. Next time we'll raise more money. Next time we'll only accept this type of applicant. The conditions to be met before tackling a new dream or venture within the church become more stringent. Sometimes our conditions for action become so narrow, we never move on.

Failure will always be a part of life; even when taking all the proper precautions we can never be absolutely sure it won't creep up and catch us in the end. In God's economy, He makes room for failure. There's room for error—space to make mistakes. These mess-ups won't surprise Him and they are not too powerful for Him to overcome. Despite what all our senses might be telling us, in God's economy, we're intended to walk out on those proverbial slender limbs.

A church committed to following the lead of the Spirit injects a risk factor into her faith. She values launching out into risky ministry based upon God's desire to bear fruit through His people and through the specific promises He has spoken to her. She values this even if failure appears to be a strong possibility. For instance, in the case of starting up MAC's roasting business, Alliance World Coffees, we knew quality coffee when we tasted it and we knew how to properly prepare coffee beverages. However, we had never attempted to roast green coffee beans. We all lacked valuable experience. And for that matter, not one of the interns possessed real-life business experience. We knew God had called the interns to learn ministry skills, and he had called me to teach them. We knew we didn't want those prepared for ministry to be weighed down by debt at the end of their training. Selling fresh-roasted coffee beans to the accounts I had through my coffee equipment business could foreseeably support a handful of interns. We knew God was able to successfully connect all the pieces to make this wild idea actually work. Perhaps He would. *Perhaps?*

In the mid-1990s, MAC very much needed more space as our original church building bulged with people whenever we opened the doors. Desperate for space, we faced another moment of decision—would we decide to play it safe or walk forward in risky faith? Most often, following God requires the latter.

In order to get a loan from the Christian & Missionary Alliance, they required us to follow a carefully constructed capital campaign. This campaign had proven successful in the past as other churches were able to raise the necessary amount to secure a loan. First, the leaders in the church were to commit to a certain amount of giving and this standard would set the tone of generosity for the rest of the church. Among other fundraising activities, over a round of intimate dinners Judy and I were to ask those in the church to make pledges, immediate gifts as well as faith gifts that would be given over the coming years. As the consultant for this capital campaign factored in MAC's general budget and the number of people attending, he projected we would raise $250,000—the necessary amount to secure a loan—if we followed the procedure he had outlined.

In the face of a building project, MAC had a choice. We could fill in the blanks of the mathematical equation set forth by experienced fund-raisers: **capital campaign** applied to **x amount of people** with **current operating budget** will yield **$250,000**. Or we could turn our backs on compelling estimations. The calculations were "tried and true" and offered some confidence as we marched into uncertain territory. If we opted out of the capital campaign, the consultant was pretty certain we would come up short in the end.

I didn't like this brand of confidence. The whole idea of playing the scripted roles of a fundraising operation felt obscene in comparison to the belief God had so deeply instilled in MAC: God wants it more than we do.

We flushed the plan. We opted for faith believing God would provide. Twice I mentioned our hopes to build onto the church building (an obvious need at the time as people in the pews were spilling into aisles and hallways), and the price this new space would cost us. I asked the church to pray about it and to respond accordingly. We never set up a special fund, we never asked for faith gifts, and we never set up a paper thermometer with rising red ink to gauge the progress toward our goal while keeping us motivated to give.

Instead of asking people to respond to my direct requests—the appeal of man—I left it up to the Holy Spirit. People responded to the Holy Spirit's prompting (and, incidently, grew in their own spiritual journeys) and gave accordingly. Any money collected was first applied toward our general budget, any surplus was set aside to fund the building project. In the end, we collected $250,000 for the addition.

Of course walking by faith toward possible failure isn't restricted to hefty financial matters. MAC displays risky behavior in the way she views those who make up the body of Christ. In other words, we take risks with people, too. Given our confidence in grassroots ministry—the Spirit can move anyone to begin a ministry at any time for anything[41]—the human tendency is to stop and ask, "Can this person do it?" If it seems likely he can't, the church stops him from trying. Instead, MAC believes in giving the body of Christ the responsibility. If a person fails, he'll learn. If he is successful, he'll learn. For instance, back when my assistant pastor Chad left to plant another church, we risked failure by asking the second-year interns—remember, these were young men who hadn't even completed the program yet—to teach some of the classes to the first-year interns. At other points in MAC's history, district leaders felt uneasy supporting the two young pastors I had picked to lead a new church. Those in authority over me stated they normally wouldn't allow such young and inexperienced pastors. However, when they observed our multi-site church and mentoring model, they understood this unique context as a place to raise and nurture pastors at a younger age.

God asks us to walk by faith, not by guarantees. If the church is following God, at some point she won't have any confidence that God will show up, bridge the gap, and safely carry her to the destination she is traveling toward. Often the only assurance a church has is the knowledge that He could do it if He decided to. Perhaps.

As it turn out, *perhaps* has biblical precedence. In 1 Samuel 14, Jonathan and his father Saul are in the midst of a war with the Philistines. As Saul reclines under a pomegranate tree, Jonathan turns to his armor bearer. "Come, let's go over to the outpost of those uncircumcised fellows. Perhaps the Lord will act in our behalf. Nothing can hinder the Lord from saving, whether by many or by few."[42]

Jonathan didn't have to go fight. He could have remained behind with his father and even defended this citing he was following the kings orders. Instead, Jonathan decided to risk it. He and his armor-bearer climbed up the rough terrain on all fours to fight the Philistines—the worst possible position for battle, both geographically and physically.

The only assurance bolstering this wildly risky decision was a flimsy two-syllable world: *perhaps.*

These two men pursued the Lord and tested Him on His ancient promise to give the Philistines over into the hands of the Israelites.[43] At MAC we're prone to say "yes" to new ministry ideas even if it appears foolhardy to do so. If these ideas fall in line with the promises God has made in His word and with the promises He has specifically made to us through the stacked deck and the spider web, there is no reason to waste time calculating the outcomes. We promptly move forward believing God is with us, in effect, testing Him.

For Jonathan and his armor-bearer, the risk paid off in the end as they defeated the Philistines. God has proven Himself faithful to the MAC community as well. He's provided numerous church-plant buildings, a larger MAC roasting facility, nearly a dozen pastors, and hundreds of worshipers to launch into new sites at the time of this writing. In general, as a church becomes comfortable with the prospect of failure, she will continually push forward into murky waters in order to discover and understand what God has for her through trial and error.

The Fear of Failure

Trial and error is a rickety platform most churches refuse to stand upon. Professional churches tend do whatever it takes to avoid a messy situation. They wait to launch new ministry ideas until they've taken the time to ensure success. The thought process looks something like this: They choose to manage the risks by identifying the outcomes, finding the probability of any negative outcomes, and then revamping the plan to reduce the uncertainty of those unwanted outcomes. If the projected success strongly outweighs any probable failure, the new ministry is given the go-ahead. These calculations are justified by the "pursuit of excellence for our Lord and Savior." Excellence, in this case, embodies strength, competence, and sureness of foot. If this is the excellence we're meant to chase, Christ would have picked different disciples.

Often the actions of the traditional church demonstrate how they fear failure as well. They rely on precedent and tradition—that which has been proven safe over the decades and even centuries. If the days of the week didn't fall on new numbers with each passing year, the pastor and parishoners of a traditional church would have no need to throw out the old church calendar. All the annual events anchor the familiar rhythm of the year while births, funerals, and weddings offer the variety. Instead of breaking away from tradition, these churches tend to trust in man's timeworn actions. "Why fix what's not broken?" they reason. "It's better to be safe than sorry." Christ beckons us, like God called Abraham, into uncharted area.

Refusing to try something new until we know we will succeed produces unbiblical effects. Valuing a standard of excellence or established precedent often stiffles creativity and encourages the fear of failure. We begin to pause upon entering a potentially messy exploit for God because the resulting outcome could be racked with faults and blemishes. Hedging against failure, churches become slow moving. The fear of failure controls the body, and they begin to risk only that which they know they cannot lose.

Hudson Taylor once said, "Unless there is an element of risk in our exploits for God, there is no need for faith."[44] He was a man intimately acquainted with risk. In 1865 he founded the China Inland Mission with the intent to reach the inland provinces of China with the Gospel while attempting to meet some of their medical needs. He required that all of his co-laborers (members of any denomination, male *or female*—a generous condition seen as borderline scandalous at the time), as well as himself, depend upon the Lord for all of their temporal needs. In other words, they were not allowed to ask for freewill offerings but instead prayerfully presented their needs to the Lord believing He would provide. Not only were his views on holy dependence radical and risky, but his missionary life was riddled with reasons to return to England, finish his medical degree, and take up private practice in safety and peace. In China he was met with a civil war, was nearly shipwrecked twice, had all his medical supplies destroyed by fire, survived a riot, was widowed twice, and lost a total of four children in China. Nevertheless, after each furlough spent in England, Hudson returned to China. His life displayed dramatic risk. By the time of his death, he had baptized over 8,000 Chinese, and 825 missionaries carried on his legacy through the China Inland Mission.[45]

If a church is left to choose between risky devotion and that of the calculated sort in the name of excellence, Christ longs for us to choose the former. Without risk there is no reason for faith. The author of Hebrews warns that "without faith it is impossible to please God."[46]

Abraham traded his extended family and the financial security of remaining in his home town for a nomadic lifestyle. For what? To set out, in faith, in search of a city whose architect and builder was God. In faith, MAC believed God wants it more than we do when we began the coffee roasting business, when we refused to do a capital campaign, and when we've appointed inexperienced laborers after seeing God use them in some small way.

Defending Against Future Failure

Watching people make silly mistakes can be painful. It is painful to see someone, especially someone who has just launched out and who is just gaining their confidence, fall flat on their face. It is even more difficult to watch someone falter and fail along the way when you challenged him to walk by faith. Weathering failure is a painful experience, but to think you pushed someone into it—that makes it difficult to sleep at night.

The general direction of every church and ministry is to become more established. Many books and seminars have delineated how Spirit-filled movements turn into organizations, organizations then turn into institutions, and institutions eventually become dead, lifeless monuments. Resisting this ultimate descent from movement to monument takes constant effort and diligence from those within a movement. Whenever a church or ministry begins to relax, we take the path of least resistance. The pain of failure produces resistance. A church relaxing into establishment will seek to cut out as much pain as they possibly can. As a result, the body of Christ becomes reactionary. Instead of proactively moving forward in risk attempting to seek out God's purposes, we fall back and insulate ourselves against pain and failure.

One defense against failure is red tape. It often strangles and holds back those who are called by the Spirit, as now they have to jump through multiple hoops before they can be obedient to the Lord's calling. People's passion and the Holy Spirit's fire are quenched at the hands of safety, policy, and trying to prevent future pain. An organism once able to easily respond to God's new plans is now mired with the bureaucratic; the organism quickly becomes an organization.

I am not saying an ideal church or ministry is policy-free. This is unreasonable. I'm not saying don't try to learn from your mistakes. That's insanity. Instead, what I am saying is this: Be wary of red tape and policies. In excess, they begin to hand the authority of the Holy Spirit over to the people. Actively look for ways to do away with needless bureaucracy. Always be moving forward; figure out the details later. You'll be surprised at how much people are willing to sacrifice when they are in the midst of a Spirit-filled movement. The thrill of the divine distracts from the temporal desires.

The Utility of Failure

I've recovered from failure; in hindsight I've realized that even though failure can damage, it also builds something into us as well.

In an earlier chapter I've shared about my brief stint in the church growth movement in the '80s. After watching Lilly Chapel, my first church, experience success across the board, I began to feel spiritually invincible. Not only had the numbers grown exponentially, but we had witnessed physical healings. Five pastors and five missionaries came from our congregation, as well as a number of new believers. I assumed God was with me because He kept blessing my church. Following this line of logic, I believed building a church in Bloomington-Normal, Illinois could be an explosive experience.

Students and young professionals had been driving from Bloomington-Normal to attend Lilly Chapel in Mackinaw, Illinois. This energetic, urban, relevant, young, and progressive group—the cream of the crop, in my mind—would jump-start the plant. This church plant had to be a sure thing.

I also assumed the demographics of the city would cater to the success of the plant. Young professionals and college students abounded, a group that is typically progressive in thought and who understand change as a norm. Working with and around these people would be an 180-degree turn from the Mayberry-mindset of Mackinaw. My ambition purred with delight: If I can build a church of 300 in the cornfields of Mackinaw, surely I could build a church of thousands in the city.

I was headed for trouble. In hindsight, I think God wanted me to be a pastor and I think He wanted to bless me, but I obviously wasn't in a place to be blessed. I had sinful ambition, and as you know, all my big plans collapsed. I endured a backbreaking load of rejection and was stripped of my ambition, the need to prove myself, my arrogance, and my pride.

Four years later, after a forced vacation from vocational ministry, I interviewed at a dying Muncie Alliance Church as a changed man. I was a pastor with a fresh dose of humility and a newfound dependence upon Christ. Standing in this new posture toward Christ, He was setting me up to learn my most important spiritual lesson to date—who the church truly belongs to and how far this truth reaches into every decision a church makes.

God uses our failures to teach us and to prepare us for His future blessing as He did through my experiences at Lilly Chapel, a failed church plant, and more recently through the organic structure at MAC. In addition to humility and dependence, God teaches us mercy through failure.

As I look back on my biggest failure, honestly, I feel God set me up to fail. I'm not the first. The disciple Peter underwent this experience as well. In the Garden of Gethsemane Jesus warns Peter that Satan has asked to sift him like wheat. Christ granted the enemy permission to do so, effactually setting Peter up to fail. That night, in an environment of fear, confusion, and accusatory questions from stangers, the enemy shook up Peter's once steadfast commitment to Jesus. Buckling under the pressure, Peter denied he ever knew Christ, not once, but three times. He recanted his devotion to his Savior—a devotion he passionately declared to Christ only hours before: "Lord, with you I am ready to go both to prison and to death!"[47]

Many times, as believers, we will think we are strong enough, gifted enough, and able enough to find success along our spiritual journeys. We have a higher opinion of ourselves than what we should. Peter claimed boldly, "Even though all may fall away because of you, I will never fall away."[48] Likewise, in my own heart I thought, *If I can build a church of 300 in a town of 1,400, what could I be capable of in a city of 100,000?*

We need to learn our limitations. We need to understand our ability to fail. Every one of us will fail—it's not a matter of *if*, but *when.*

During these failures, we can either lose faith and allow bitterness to take root in its stead, or we can learn mercy. Of course, Christ wants us to learn mercy. He explicity told the Pharises so. "But go and learn what this means: 'I desire mercy, and not sacrifice,' for I did not come to call the righteous, but sinners."[49]

Christ always knew Peter would turn his back on him—even though this probably took Peter by surprise. But Christ has confidence in His people. He knew Peter would turn again, and when he did,

Christ commanded him to strengthen his brothers and sisters. And the most effective way to encourage the body of Christ would be through the lens of mercy—not through self-importance and a spotless spiritual track record. Peter turned out to be a better pastor because of his failure.

So often, Christians believe that one failure disqualifies them from ever contributing to the body in the future. After Peter's embarrassing showing the night of Christ's arrest, he returned to the fishing business. In his mind, he obviously wasn't cut out for service in the spiritual community. In fact, that's why he went into fishing in the first place. Jewish boys who underperformed in their education eventually took up their father's business. This is what happened to Peter. Instead of continuing his studies under a rabbi with the intent to become a rabbi himself, he learned the fishing trade.

After blowing it with Jesus, Peter sensibly reacquainted himself with a boat and fishing gear. One morning, a man appeared on the banks of the Sea of Galilee. He called out:

"Catching any fish today?"

"No," Peter dejectedly answered as the other disciples who had followed him to the waterfront shook their heads.

Playing the role of a first-century equivalent of a back seat driver, the man suggested: "Why don't you cast the net on the right side of the boat?"[50]

Patronizing the bystander, they threw the nets over the other side. With nets so full of fish, the men couldn't haul them back into the boat. This stranger on the shore had unmistakably recreated the moment when Christ first called Peter to follow Him. The familiarity of the scene snapped their eyes into focus and they knew the man standing before them on the sandy beach was not a stranger, but the resurrected Christ. Peter hurriedly jumped off the boat and swam ashore while his companions followed behind.

After finishing a breakfast of fresh fish, Jesus fixed his eyes on Peter, "Simon, son of John, do you love Me?"

"Yes, Lord; You know that I love you."

"Tend my lambs."

Christ initiates the exhange a second time, Peter professes his love, and again Christ commands Peter to shepherd his sheep. A third time, He questions Peter's devotion, to which Peter repeats his original response. Jesus replies, "Tend my sheep."

Three times Peter denied Christ, but Christ does not condemn him. In His mercy, He allows Peter to reaffirm his love, as if to undo each of his mess-ups, and in response to Peter's declared devotion, three times Jesus reinstates Peter's call to ministry.

Jesus could now entrust His people into Peter's hands because he would show mercy. He would cut believers some slack as they lived out and faltered through the Christian life. Fast-forwarding to the end of Peter's life, notice his merciful encouragement to the Christians who were in the throes of Nero's systematic persecution:

> To the elders among you...shepherd the flock...exercising oversight not under compulsion...not for sordid gain, but...be examples to the flock. All of you clothe yourselves with humility towards one another...that He may exalt you at the proper time. Be alert. Your adversary, the devil, prowls around like a roaring lion, seeking someone to devour. But resist him, firm in your faith. After you have suffered for a little while...the God of all grace will perfect, confirm, strengthen, and establish you. (2 Peter 5:1-10, paraphrased)

In God's economy, failure isn't feared and loathed as it is in our modern churches. When Christ commanded the Pharisees to go and learn mercy, He was offering them the chance to find true and holy leadership within a spiritual community. We'll never know if some of these men did as Jesus commanded; the Bible never offers their narrative. However, Peter's story is written out for our instruction. Peter went and failed. Through the process he learned mercy. Instead of his failure disqualifying him, ironically it qualified and prepared him for service within the body.

• • •

Despite the worth and purpose that can be found in failure, the church won't fail every time we try something risky. A risky endeavor can turn out to be a gleaming success just like it did for Jonathan and his armor bearer. Not only were the Philistines defeated that day, but also the people of God rallied, unified, and experienced a renewed faith.

After climbing up on their hands and feet, Jonathan and his armor bearer defeated nearly twenty men. The earth began to tremble and the multitide of Philistines began to retreat. This caught King Saul's attention, as well as everyone else back at camp. God had turned the tide of the battle in their favor, and they jumped up to join in. Then those who had defected to the enemy noticed God's presence with their countrymen, and they began fighting the Philistines from within. Finally, when the men hiding in caves heard the Philistines were retreating, they left safety and pursued their enemies to defeat.[51]

In time, taking a risk often creates a domino effect of once-skeptic believers falling in line with the movement of God. Initially, some may struggle to understand or believe God would lead the church in a risky direction, but as they witness Him showing up, bridging the gap, and connecting the pieces, they join the fray. The church is united and focused under a purpose of God.

Taking risks in the face of possible failure creates a climate of freedom in a church. The body, unshackled by the fear of failure or the pressure to succeed walks by faith into uncharted area. Failure—rather than causing the community to shrink back, lay low in shame, and languish in stagnancy—teaches humility, dependence, and mercy, and is viewed as a natural byproduct of moving forward in search of the purposes God has for His church. A church displaying this sort of atmosphere has given back the church and opened the door for Jesus to come in. She becomes a place where His people can experience the thrill of the divine.

Questions for Reflection

1. How has the pursuit of excellence quenched emerging work of the Spirit?

2. What past failures have created apprehension so that you find it harder to risk following God in the present? List the past hurts that paralyzed you today.

3. How have you seen failure prepare people for future fruitfulness?

Chapter 10

Giving Permission

Have you ever heard the following argument between siblings? Mom or Dad hands out twenty-five cents each to two young children. Each looks in their hand, delighted with the cold hard cash. Delighted, that is, until they look into the hand of their sibling. One has two dimes and a nickel, the other a quarter.

"Not fair! Why did you give him more?" To make matters worse, the sibling with three coins smiles haughtily.

Then there's the game of copycat that inevitably surfaces on boring road trips.

"My friend Suzy has five dogs," one announces for no particular reason.

"*My friend Suzy has five dogs,*" the other mocks.

"You don't have a friend named Suzy!"

"*You don't have a friend named Suzy...*"

"You're just saying what I'm saying."

"*You're just saying what I'm saying.*"

"Stop repeating me!"

"*Stop repeating me!*"

"Mom!"

Tattle-tale.

Too often, I see these same sort of antics in the church. In so many ways we're not the strong, confident bride God desires us to be. At least, not yet.

Comparison Complex

God warns His children about comparing ourselves against others and their ministries. In the Corinthian church, false apostles introduced this fleshly attitude of comparison. They compared themselves to Paul in hopes of undermining him. They pointed out that while they had letters of recommendation from important people, Paul had none. Secondly, when he wrote to the Corinthians his letters were weighty and strong, but in person his presence was unimpressive and his speech poor.[52]

Paul strikes down this destructive attitude. "For we are not bold to class or compare ourselves with some of those who commend themselves; but when they measure themselves by themselves and compare themselves with themselves, they are without understanding."[53] Paul further explains how there are definite and fixed spaces God apportions to each of His children in which their power of influence is confined. God made Paul the master builder and it was futile for these false apostles to claim the church as their own; they were merely scavengers desiring the success of another man's God-given territory.[54]

Paul had already explained the following to the Corinthians: "Now there are varieties of gifts, but the same Spirit. And there are varieties of ministries, but the same Lord. There are varieties of effects, but the same God who works all things in all persons."[55] In other words, the Holy Spirit imparts specific spiritual gifts to His children; ministries are the sphere or the territory in which the gift operates; and the effect is the power of that gift working itself out in one's territory. These three elements working together define a person's capacity. For instance, one could have the gift of evangelism. The gift could be interpersonal and deal with writing to a friend or it could play out in something completely different like a very noticeable Billy Graham crusade. Wherever and however the gift is used is the sphere in which your gift works: your ministry. The effect of that gift within the proper sphere is brought about by the power of God. The bottom line is: God gives each of His children a certain capacity and He is faithful to grow us into our specific capacity as we are faithful.

On the contrary, many churches today have a comparison complex. We observe our successful peers and want the same thing for ourselves. We dream that maybe we could be the next fill-in-the-blank with the famous-church-of-the-moment. We want the staggering numbers, the uber-cool vibe, the far-reaching influential platform. Again, these desires can be justified by the progress of the Gospel, but why do we put those expectations on ourselves? God has portioned His grace out in specific and thoughtful ways. It's pointless to try to stretch our capacity beyond what God intends. Do we really think we can become something other than what God has determined for us?

Just like the servants in Matthew 25:15, He gives some five talents, some two talents, some one—each to his own ability. Let God give what He is going to give. He sees all, He knows all, and He has the common good in mind.[56] Besides, the two faithful servants, regardless of how they performed against each other, both received the same reward in the end.

Within each local body of Christ there are unique people with distinctive talents, strengths, and tendencies. There is an infinite amount of ways God can bring about His fruit within His body. He has something unique He wants to work in the midst of His followers and He will faithfully bring it about. If we follow Him, then we as believers will live up to Paul's strong words in 2 Corinthians 10:17-18. "But he who boasts is to boast in the Lord. For it is not he who commends himself that is approved, but he whom the Lord commends."

Copy Cats

People traffic through MAC all the time examining our internship program, the ways we have married business and ministry, and our multi-site model. After hundreds of meetings with interested persons, our church model gives some the permission to be and to do something unique; we authenticate God's creative work in their church. Others come searching for a program to insert into their own church. It's maddening to watch a church try to be something they aren't naturally—they are wasting time. If after reading this book you decide the way to go is to start up a multi-site church with bi-vocational staff and a ministry training program that is funded by an in-house coffee roasting business, you've missed the point entirely.

In this walk of faith, as we learn to become a healthy, functioning body of Christ, there is no formula, there are no "to do" lists, there are no easy answers—and if someone says otherwise, this Nimrod is trying to sell you something. In this walk of faith, as we learn to become a body of Christ, there will be struggle, confusion, and more questions as we continue along our journey.

However, there is something valuable and long-lasting embedded in struggle. If the life of Abraham failed to illumine this truth for you, look to the children of Israel. After wandering in the desert with Moses for forty years, Joshua led Israel into the Promised Land. Thanks to the works of God and Joshua's leadership, the nation kept its focus on the Lord. This generation saw the waters of the Jordan River—during flood season—recede and pile up so that they could cross. They saw the walls of Jericho come tumbling down. They battled intimidating enemies and were victorious. Nevertheless, this generation grew old and eventually passed away. In Judges 2:7 we find their collective epitaph: "The people served the Lord all the days of Joshua and all the days of the elders who survived Joshua, who had seen all the great work of the Lord which He had done for Israel."

With such a great heritage, wouldn't you expect the next generation to follow their example? That's not what happened. Through the narrative of Judges, we see how the subsequent generations needed to experience the Lord for themselves. The generation following Joshua's did not know the Lord or experience the work He had done for Israel. As a result they spiraled into sin, aimlessness, and paltry spirituality, as the book of Judges tells us.[57] The stories of God's work during the lives of their mothers and fathers failed to move them. History was something that happened to someone else and the relevance was lost on the subsequent generations.

The church cannot thrive on the adopted struggles, lessons, plans, and actions of other churches. Just as they did for the children of Israel, eventually others' stories and testimonies of the work of God will lose their poignancy, and their power will be lost on us. We must see the Lord for ourselves.

I feel sorry for pastors who run off to a seminar to pick up a vision. I know pastors are under pressure to perform, so it's supremely difficult to sit back and wait for God to move. The temptation is to run after a successful vision—and there is an abundance of nice, neat programs packaged and priced for such a need as this. But sometimes it's best to remain at home. Trust that Jesus will show up and make things happen when we step back and stop driving the body of Christ. We crowd out God when we install programs to prop up the body.

God has specifically gifted each and every man, woman, and child in the church. Taking into account the different personalities, propensities, talents, and strengths of these people, the possibilities for unique and creative ministries are certainly endless. Each church can experience God in its own tailor-made adventure.

God will use our natural inclinations, giftings, and interests for His ministry. When you are drawn to something—even something as mundane as coffee—don't write it off as some silly interest. God has thoughtfully written these desires across our hearts. Years ago He told me to "do what I put within you to do" through the analogy of the spider web. Who would have guessed that my simple inclination for really good coffee would be paired with something as lofty as God's unfolding purposes?

But it was.

A simple interest in coffee fostered a natural connection to purchase a coffee roaster to fund an internship program. Darren, who doesn't even drink coffee, was interested in the book business in his early twenties. As his business expanded, he opened new stores. Each time, he hired me to install an espresso bar, and he bought some of his beans from Alliance World Coffees. Every pound of AWC coffee funds our ministries. This is just one example of overlap we didn't plan years ago when the Spirit led us off the beaten path. The business world would call this synergy. We just chalk it up to God's creativity and His incapability to waste a single person, desire, or possibility. If we stay out of God's way, His promises and desires will fully come to pass. In the process we will know God. Among other things, we won't be telling second-hand stories.

The Wise Old Man

At some point in our spiritual journeys we've all acted childishly. I've compared myself to others, only to despair or feel a false sense of superiority. I've mimicked others in hopes of joining in their own success. When we falter, whether it is once or many times over, God doesn't throw up His hands in exasperation and give up on us.

This is not God's nature.

The truth of this statement is seen in a special image my friend Chad once saw in one of our prayer meetings:

A young man walked into a quiet room where a wise, old man busily worked at his writing desk. The visitor watched him work for a few minutes. He noticed the old man smiled as he wrote; sometimes he laughed. His happy demeanor influenced the young man so strongly that he found himself joining in on the laughter without even knowing what was so funny. The joy in the room beckoned him forward until, quite boldly, the youth began to read over the writer's shoulder. The scratch of pen to paper never ceased and slowly, the man noticed a familiar sequence of events. In surprised awe, he laughed in spite of himself. The old man was writing the young man's life story. Reading along, he began to prompt the writer. This must have been supremely annoying, but he simply nodded in response and evenly continued. The young man began to grow impatient—though he tried to appear as though the old man's slow pace didn't bother him.

Sensing his anxiety, the old man looked at him and paused—for just a moment. As silence fell upon the room the young man eagerly grabbed the pen and furiously began to write.

The old man looked unphased as the pages slid away from him. He adjusted his glasses, leaned his head on his hand, and began to read over the young man's shoulder.

The novice writer continued steadily along as the old man contentedly enjoyed himself. The man became more daring with his twists and turns of the plot. At the peak of the young man's showiness, the old man gave a very gratifying, yet sincere belly laugh.

But as he continued, he became less sure about the ending—even though the wise man's confidence never seemed to wane. Slowly, writing became less appealing as the story line became unfocused and muddled. He had written himself into a corner and wasn't sure how to tie up all the loose ends. He desperately wanted a good ending but wasn't sure it could be done.

Embarassed, the young man set the pen down and moved to crumple up the sheets of paper. The old man caught his hand. Smiling his confident smile, he slid the papers back in front of himself. Never crossing out a passage or struggling as to where to begin, the pen began to evenly scratch against the paper.

Effortlessly, he incorporated the young man's missteps and ambition into his own writing. As time passed the jumbled mess began to right itself into a coherent resolution. As the wise, old man approached the end of the final page, the story finished in a beautiful, unique ending, to the young man's delight.

God wants it more than we do.

Questions for Reflection

1. What has God written upon your heart?

2. Talk about times when you took the pen.

3. Talk about when you gave it back.

MINISTRY MODELS

 Professional Model
Pastor as CEO

 Traditional Model
Pastor as Chaplain

 Organic/Movement Model
Pastor as Equipper

Professional Model
Pastor as CEO

Ministry Philosophy

- Adopted From Corporate World
- Driven by Corporate Vision
- Top-down Driven

Ministry Values

Leadership

- Professional Driven
- Hire By Qualifications
- Ladder Climbing Mentality
- Hire Someone Trained
- Staffing for Programs

Decision Making

- Changes Made at Staff Meetings
- Calculating and Study Opportunities
- Policy Driven
- Garnished in Prayer

Resources

- Budget Centered
- Capital Campaign

Ministry Practice

Vision

- Program Focus
- Empowering through Job Description
- Create/Import Programs to Accomplish Vision

Image

- Concerned with Appearing Strong
- Slick and Successful
- Value Higher Education
- Value Perfection

Structure

- Organization Oriented
- Meeting Centered
- Planned/Flow Chart Focused

Opportunities

- Calculate & Control the Risk
- Determined by Staff
- Policy Oriented
- Vertical Growth

Traditional Model
Pastor as Chaplain

Ministry Philosophy

- Adopted From Democratic Process
- Traditional or Congregational Vision
- Bottom-Up Driven

Ministry Values

Leadership

- Congregation Driven
- Hire for Church Needs
- Election Mentality
- Study by Committee
- Staffing for Maintenance
- Seek Volunteers
- Pastor Seen as a Hireling

Decision Making

- Changes Made by Committees/ Congregation
- Follow Traditions
- Red Tape
- Garnished in Prayer

Resources

- Budget Centered
- Wills and Trusts

Ministry Practice

Vision

- Follow Congregational Traditions
- Church Focused

Image

- Concerned with Appearing Strong
- Value Service from Pastor
- Professional

Structure

- Institutional Structure
- Congregation Orientation
- Church Tradition
- By Churches Needs

Opportunities

- Run From Risk
- Maintaining Equilibrium
- Church Focused
- Status Quo

Organic/Movement Model
Pastor as Equipper

Ministry Philosophy

- Comes from the New Testament Model
- Grass Roots Driven
- "Chazon" Vision of Christ

Ministry Values

Leadership

- Staffing for Outreach & Mission
- Trust God to Stir & Raise Up
- Recognize & Release Mentality
- Grass Roots Directed
- Ministry by Function
- Homegrown Staff

Decision Making

- Changes by those Called
- Ministry Birthed in Prayer
- Audience of One
- Risk Oriented

Resources

- Budget is a Guideline
- Pray and Trust
- Faith Centered

Vision

- Ministry Carried out by those Called
- Train those Called & Stirred
- Demonstrate & Model
- Outreach Focused

Image

- Embrace Failures & Weaknesses
- Movement Oriented
- Audience of One

Structure

- Organism Structured
- Relational
- Movement Based

Opportunities

- Take & Embrace Risk
- Expansion Focused
- Lateral Growth

Endnotes

Chapter 1

1. Paraphrased from Acts 20:28, 29. Unless otherwise noted, all scripture quotations are from the NASB.

Chapter 2

2. Genesis 11:4
3. Genesis 11:6
4. Genesis 15:7. At this point in scripture, Abraham's name is actually Abram—God has not added the suffix "ha" to his birthname. However, for simplicity, we will always refer to Abram by Abraham.
5. Emphasis added to note use of *para*.
6. Scripture taken from *The Message*.
7. Exodus 3:11
8. Isaiah 6:3
9. Isaiah 6:5, paraphrased
10. Genesis 12:3; 15:5, 16
11. 2 Chronicles 20:7, Isaiah 41:8, James 2:23, Genesis 15:1.
12. Hebrews 11:16
13. Revelation 3:17
14. Hebrews 11:14-16
15. 2 Corinthians 4:17

Chapter 3

16. At this point in scripture, God has not changed Sarai's name to Sarah. For reasons of simplicity, we will always refer to Sarai as Sarah.

Chapter 4

17. Luke 10:38
18. Acts 13:23, Hebrews 2:10
19. John 8:3
20. Matthew 26:46

Chapter 5

21. Revelations 3:17
22. Revelations 3:18

Chapter 6

23. Genesis 15:6
24. Genesis 15:8
25. Genesis 15:18
26. Genesis 16
27. This term was originally coined by Frank Tillapaugh in his book *Unleashing the Church*; Regal Books, 1982, page 51.
28. Ephesians 3:20

Chapter 7

29. NIV, emphasis added.
30. Luke 1:38, NIV
31. Luke 1:38, NIV
32. Luke 1:45
33. Luke 1:42-43

Chapter 8

34. NIV
35. John 5:19, NIV (emphasis added)
36. Acts 4:13, NIV
37. Acts 1:8, NIV
38. 1 Timothy 1:18
39. 1 Timothy 4:14
40. 1 Timothy 1:18; 4:14.

Chapter 9

41. within the values of the church
42. 1 Samuel 14:6, NIV
43. Deuteronomy 7:22-24
44. Hudson Taylor, source unknown
45. J. Husdon Taylor, Hudson Taylor (Bloomington, Minn.: Bethany House Publishers, 1987) 16,17, 54, 59-61. Janet and Geoff Benge, Hudson Taylor: Deep in the Heart of China (Seattle, Wash.: Youth with a Mission Publishing, 1998) 131, 155, 175, 186, 196-197, 199, 203-204.
46. Hebrews 11:6, NIV
47. Luke 22:33
48. Matthew 26:33
49. Matthew 9:13
50. John 21:4-8
51. 1 Samuel 14:20-23

Chapter 10

52. 2 Corinthians 3:1, 10:10
53. 2 Corinthians 10:12
54. 1 Corinthians 3:10-17
55. 1 Corinthians 12:4-6
56. 1 Corinthians 12:7
57. Judge 2:10

FOR MORE INFORMATION

For more information about the ministries and businesses discussed in this book, check out the following websites.

Muncie Alliance Church
It's where the stacked deck all began. MAC is a multiplication training center and home base for interns, laity, pastors, and businesses. Visit www.munciealliance.org.

Movement of Alliance Communities
A group of churches who study together, do missions together, and contribute five percent  of their incomes to planting new churches within the MAC movement. For more information, you can check us out at www.alliancemovement.com.

Guido's Coffee and Espresso Equipment
Looking for professional-grade coffee bar equipment? Since 1992, Guy and Judy Pfanz have helped open or add espresso bars to more than two hundred locations. Check out Guido's Coffee and Espresso Equipment at www.guidoscoffee.com.

Coffee Video Magazine
An informational and educational video-format online magazine

related to all things coffee. Coffee Video Magazine also specializes in film and video production services for companies in the specialty coffee industry. Visit us at www.coffeevideomagazine.com.

Alliance World Coffees

Alliance World Coffees is a church-owned coffee-roasting company established to support students training for ministry. You'll find some of the best coffee at www.awcoffees.com.

The Coffee Institute

The Coffee Institute is an intensive coffee-training school that focuses on excellence and hands-on comprehension. We offer a wide range of crucial topics from basic barista skills and shop management to advanced-level barista training and concepts for high end shops. Come join us for a three-day barista training or a six-day course focused on opening a coffee shop. Find course schedules and register online at www.thecoffeeinstitute.com.

Stacking the Deck

If you would like to purchase more books or are interested in booking Guy as a speaker, please visit www.stackingthedeckthebook.com.

Stay tuned for...

Vecinos Coffee Gallery

Vecinos Coffee Gallery is a trademarked coffee shop and turnkey package available for purchase. See what it's all about at www.vecinoscoffeegallery.com.

1 Take Live

1 Take Live is a video production company specializing in recording live concerts in a 500-seat music venue. More information is available at www.1takelive.com.

ACKNOWLEDGMENTS

As I read this book before it goes to print, I realize the perfect goodness of the Father who brings wonderful insight to us in difficult times. He made the promise of the spider web and stacked deck during my most painful times of rejection. He changed my perspective and gave me hope for what seemed like the most uncertain of times. As I contemplated the spider weaving such a wonderful piece of art and the experiences of my life up to that point, I realized that someone greater than myself was shaping my life. He also used others to give me permission to do the things God had put within me to do and to shape my emerging values.

I appreciate those people as well. Through Chuck Smith of Calvary Chapel I learned the love of teaching the whole counsel of God by teaching through scripture, book by book.

Bob Fulton taught me how to recognize God's voice and provided a way for the gifts to be released in the laity.

Frank Tillipaugh gave me the passion to become outward-focused in an organic way.

I also learned to trust a denomination. The Christian and Missionary Alliance has supported me and blessed MAC to follow the unconventional ministry ideas described in this book.

A special thanks for our Muncie Alliance family who are the beginning of the stacked deck as it now spreads to different parts of the world.

To the teaching pool guys—the current pastors at each location and the emerging guys ready to launch—doing life and ministry together has been great!

As God promised, He continues to stack the deck. Mike Fentz, from Muncie Alliance, sketched all the interior art work. Thanks for sharing your talent with us. Lindsay Conner, from The Mercy House (one of our site churches in Anderson, Indiana), edited our manuscript. Check out her site at www.word-out.com. Mary Jaracz, also from The Mercy House, designed our cover and layout. She'd love to layout your book! You can contact her at: marij4@gmail.com.

Monica sends out her love and thanks to her family, Jeanette, Lisa, Meagan, Sadee, as well as Mark and Andrea whose encouragement prodded her along, to Nicola who selflessly gave of her time, and to her steadfast husband Shawn, the leader of the pack on both fronts.

Monica, thanks for your patience and all the rewrites.

And finally, my wife Judy. You have loyally stood by me through the constant change and expansion of many new businesses that have developed and facilitated the multiplication of ministry. Thank you.

About the Authors

A thirty-year veteran pastor, Guy Pfanz is the senior pastor of Muncie Alliance Church (MAC), a multi-site church with six sister sites. Forced into bi-vocational ministry early on at MAC, he and his wife Judy currently own and operate Guido's Coffee and Espresso Equipment, a full-service specialty coffee equipment provider. An avid entrepreneur, Pfanz has founded Alliance World Coffees, Coffee Video Magazine, and The Coffee Institute. Each of these businesses either fund

or fully support ministry. Other businesses in the works include Vecinos Coffee Gallery, 1 Take Live, and a wedding chapel church plant.

Monica Hoover is a freelance writer living in Indianapolis with her husband Shawn. She graduated from Indiana University and is part of the stacked deck within the Movement of Alliance Communities.